GHOSTS AND PHANTOMS OF THE WEST

C000048195

Peter Underwood
FRSA

BOSSINEY BOOKS

First published in 1993 by Bossiney Books, St Teath, Bodmin, Cornwall.

Typeset and printed by Penwell Ltd, Callington, Cornwall

ISBN 0 948158 87 5

ACKNOWLEDGEMENTS

Front cover photography: ROY WESTLAKE
Back cover photography: RAY BISHOP
Front cover design: MAGGIE GINGER

About the Author – and the book

PETER UNDERWOOD *has been President of the Ghost Club (founded 1862) since 1960 and has probably heard more first-hand ghost stories than any man alive. A long-standing member of* The Society for Psychical Research, *Vice-President of the Unitarian Society for Psychical Studies, a member of* The Folklore Society, The Dracula Society *and a former member of the Research Committee of the Psychic Research Organisation, he has lectured, written and broadcast extensively. In 1987 he was elected a Fellow of the Royal Society of Arts.*

He took part in the first official investigation into a haunting; has sat with physical and mental mediums, and conducted investigations at seances, been present at exorcisms, experiments at dowsing, precognition, clairvoyance, hypnotism, regression; conducted world-wide tests in telepathy and extra-sensory perception, and has personally investigated scores of haunted houses.

This is his ninth title for Bossiney. His publications for the Cornish cottage publishers include Ghostly Encounters *and* Westcountry Hauntings. *In these, his latest investigations, Peter Underwood writes of cases which transcend all known laws. He has been called 'Britain's ghost hunter supreme' and 'the undisputed king of ghost hunters.' The following pages are an opportunity to join him on the ghost hunting trail.*

4

HAUNTINGS
AND HABITATIONS

GHOSTS and phantoms of the West are varied: enchanting and frightening, attractive and repulsive, quiet and noisy – but never tedious.

Some idea of the variety of reported ghostly activity can be judged by looking at just one haunted category: Inns.

There is a ghost cat at the *Lion and Flag* at Blagdon Hill near Taunton; heavy footsteps and movement of objects at *The Plough*, Bere Ferrers in Devon; five ghosts who switch furniture around and interfere with people in bed at *The Crown* at Pewsey, Wiltshire; a ghostly young man in teddy boy gear at *The Boot* at Weymouth, Dorset; a Lady in Grey in one bedroom and a disembodied voice in another at *The Bear* at Chippenham, Wiltshire; a headless woman at *The Phoenix*, Pewsey; a ghost child, accidentally burned to death there, causes a scar on the arms of those who see her at *The Bridge*, West Lavington, Wiltshire; there is a ghost monk at *The King and Queen* at High Worth near Swindon; a friendly ghost in a bedroom at *The Wellington*, Boscastle, Cornwall that appears to caress living animals; and the ghost of a murdered Spanish merchant at *The Plough* at Holford in Somerset.

But ghosts that haunt inns and hotels have acquired something of a bad name for they tend to attract visitors and sometimes the stories became exaggerated; not that I would discount all reportedly haunted inns, for hostelries are in a way the perfect microcosm of human life. They are frequented by all manner of people in all sorts of circumstances and they are mute witnesses to all sorts of happenings.

It is more than likely that some of these happenings remain recorded on the atmosphere at an inn as well as at a haunted manor house, a cottage or farmhouse; and fascinating stories about hauntings affecting all such habitations are to be found here with witnesses of outstanding quality, people like Stanbury Thompson,

■ *The Wellington with its friendly bedroom ghost ...*

BA, Rosemary Pollock, Reg Wickens, Lady Burnett-Stuart and Colonel John Blashford-Snell, MBE, to mention only a few.

So come with me to wild Wiltshire, the leafy lanes of Devon, the solitude of Somerset, enchanted Cornwall, delightful Dorset and unforgettable Avon – all have their ghosts and phantoms; all have their individual tugs on our heartstrings; their special characteristics; their unforgettableness for they are all part of the magic that is the Westcountry.

Peter Underwood
Savage Club
1 Whitehall Place
London SW1A 2HD

The large man
Bath, Avon

I HAVE a letter from film executive Anthony Sutherland of Hove, dated April, 1980 and I quote:

'… the following is a true story, as God is my witness. It was in 1962 and I was in Bath casting a film for the Rank organisation called 80,000 Suspects. It was winter and I recall that the snow was deep, in fact Bath was cut off with drifts of six to eight feet blocking the main roads. At first I put up at a hotel next to the station, but I soon had to leave as the hotel switchboard became constantly jammed with calls from local people who wanted to be film extras.

'I found refuge in a very old Victorian house in Lansdowne Road, where there was a fine baronial hall and a minstrel gallery – and I made a mental note to use the place in a film one day. Even before I knew anything of the history of the house or its inhabitants and had had no experiences, both my late wife and I felt that we were being constantly watched; there was an expectant, waiting atmosphere about the place.

'Mrs Hale owned the house and she was a dear old lady who lived there all alone with her little dog. I had already engaged her as one of the film extras because of the careworn features that added character to the face, a face so full of individuality and wisdom, and singular eyes that at times had a haunted look; a look as if there was another person in the room apart from the three of us, another person whom she could see.

'I did not have long to wait before I gained my first experience of – what? A soul that could not rest? A wandering spirit? A haunting ghost? It was the third evening of our stay in that house and I was busy on the telephone getting together people who were to attend a dancing audition the following day for one of the scenes in the film. Mrs Hale was going out that evening to do charity work and my wife and I were going out to dinner after I had completed the work in hand, which I expected to be around eight o'clock. It was arranged that we would leave the key in the porchway when we went out so that Mrs Hale could let herself in; however it was nearly ten o'clock by the time I had finished and we elected to stay at

Lansdown Crescent, Bath: in such a property, film executive Anthony Sutherland had several terrifying experiences of a ghostly nature. (Photo: Bath City Council dept of leisure and tourism.)

home, and have an early night. We had a heavy day ahead.

'This required us putting the key out for Mrs Hale, but when I went to open the door I found it was locked. Although my wife and I were the only people in the house all evening, the two big and heavy doors were locked – from the inside! I unlocked the doors but still the doors would not open. I then noticed that there was a bolt about twelve inches long, holding the door shut fast. I slid the bolt back, only to find that not only was this bolt pushed firmly into the floor but also another heavy bolt at the top of the door was bolted tight. I am five feet and ten inches in height but I well recall that I had to stand on a chair in order to release the top bolt, such was the size of those doors. Next day Mrs Hale was as puzzled as we had been and we never found an explanation.

'Later that night I was pulled completely from my bed by my left arm and I was held horizontally, supported only by the calves of my legs on the side of the bed while an unknown but powerful force gripped my left wrist. Nothing of that sort had ever happened to me before; I was terrified and I can still see the look of disbelief on the face of my wife as I lay there suspended in mid-air for what must have been every second of two minutes. Then, as suddenly as it had grasped me, the tight grip released me and I fell to the floor.

'That was just the start of many happenings during my six weeks stay in that interesting house and to record everything that happened would nearly fill a book! There were footprints in the snow leading across the garden which measured some fifteen inches long and yet only made an imprint of about half-an-inch. The snow at that time was about four feet deep in the garden and when I went to investigate, I sank in up to my thighs. After this and other events, equally puzzling and never explained, I witnessed my first and only sighting of the enormous ghostly man that haunted the house; but during my stay in Bath I met others who claimed that they too had seen the ghost of a very large man in the vicinity of the house in Lansdowne Road.

'I was later told by Mrs Hale, somewhat reluctantly, I may say, that her husband had died in the house a few years previously – cursing his family because he did not want to die. He was a very large man.'

* * * * *

The haunted tunnel
Bincombe, Dorset

THE Bincombe railway tunnel, a few miles south of Dorchester, has long been regarded as haunted. All through the days of steam trains dozens of unfortunate and unhappy men and women committed suicide by throwing themselves in front of approaching trains but there seems to to have been a higher than average number of such deaths in Bincombe tunnel. As recently as 1987 a commuter thought he would take a short cut through the tunnel when he thought he had missed his train; unfortunately the train was running late and he was killed in the 'tunnel of ill repute' as it used to be known.

In 1991 no less than four separate train drivers experienced seemingly inexplicable happenings and one saw what seems to have been a phantom form in the tunnel. That particular driver said afterwards, 'I distinctly saw someone walking towards the train! There was nothing I could do and the train must have gone straight through him; yet nothing resembling human remains were ever found afterwards.'

Another train driver told a similar story, although he was unaware at the time that anything of the kind had been reported previously. He said: 'I was approaching Bincombe tunnel, a stretch of line that has become very familiar to me, when I thought I saw something in the mouth of the tunnel. The next moment I could make out the shape of a man and he was just standing there as the train raced towards him. His clothes many have been rather old-fashioned but I was amazed that he didn't attempt to get out of the way. I closed my eyes and it was all over; nothing. I reported the incident but nothing was found; nothing at all – but I know what I saw.'

Other experienced and long-serving train drivers have reported sounds they have been unable to explain. One said he was just approaching the Bincombe tunnel when: 'I heard this thumping and crashing which appeared to be coming from outside the train; but there was nothing to account for it; it was completely unfathomable ...'

Yet another driver said he had also heard odd noises and seen 'strange shapes' on the line – and usually on a Friday night. 'That night there is often lots of thumping and banging all the way through the tunnel,' he said.

A regular commuter on the line, David Coulman, has also reported inexplicable sounds but very different ones from those reported by the train drivers and apparently originating within the train itself.

He said: 'I know it's not the Orient Express and you are bound to get some riff-raff on the train but the line must be drawn somewhere – or at least I think it should.

'It was when we were going through the tunnel that I heard the giggling, moaning and whisperings coming from the toilets. When it went on and on I decided to confront the culprits so I got up and stood outside the toilet. The sounds had stopped when we came out of the tunnel and I waited several moments before knocking on the door. It opened as I touched it and it was empty.'

My old friend Antony D. Hippisley Coxe, author of the monumental *Haunted Britain* (1973) referred to Dorchester, three miles to the north as 'the hub of an area which is full of mystery'; he may well have been more accurate than he knew.

■ *Delightful Dorset … a county of ghosts and phantoms.*

The love nest
Bournemouth, Dorset

LANGTRY Manor Hotel in Derby Road, East Cliff, has long been haunted by the ghost of Lillie Langtry (1853-1929), as well it might be for this romantic house was once her home and called The Red House.

Lillie, the attractive mistress of Edward VII when he was Prince of Wales, was known in London Society as 'Jersey Lily'. The Prince was completely fascinated by her and at the height of their romance in 1877 he built this house for her; the house where her ghost has been reportedly seen on many occasions: in the room with the heart-shaped corner bath that was once Lillie's bedroom; in the magnificent suite designed by Lillie for her prince; in the kitchen area, regularly about 4pm a few years ago; in the form of a grey female figure that glides through the house (particularly the hall and the kitchen); and her ghostly carriage has been heard and seen drawing up in the driveway of the house in the early hours.

The ghost of the Prince of Wales has also reportedly been seen in a downstairs room of the house that is now an excellent hotel. Soon after he had built the house for her, Lillie upset her royal lover by putting ice down his back at a public reception and before long she met Edward's young nephew, Prince Louis of Battenberg (father of Lord Louis Mountbatten) who wanted to marry her. Their romance flourished in Bournemouth and eventually a daughter was born, who grew up to become the mother of Mary Malcolm, one of the first women television announcers. She said fifteen years ago that she could just remember seeing 'the grand old lady' who was Lillie Langtry, in London. Mary's mother grew up believing that Edward was her father but on her marriage her mother told her it was in fact Prince Louis.

A television series depicting the Edwardian beauty and the royal romance a few years ago seemed to spark off a series of unexplained incidents at the hotel. These included a tapestry falling – or being pushed – noisily off a wall during the broadcasting of one episode.

Mrs Pamela Hamilton-Howard, the managing director, reported

Langtry Manor, built by Edward VII for Lillie Lantry.

at the time that during the transmission of the first episode she and others heard the 'most terrific thud' as the tapestry in its heavy frame fell to the ground. There was no one near at the time and the wall fastening was still firm and secure in the wall and the chain which held the tapestry was unbroken.

Mrs Hamilton-Howard explained: 'We had always believed that Lillie herself made the tapestry and, who knows, her spirit might have been trying to send us a message … odd things have certainly happened here since the television series about Lillie …'

A leading local spiritualist, Mr Albert White of Strouden Park, said it was 'quite a common occurrence for astral beings to make some gesture, such as knocking down a picture, to show they are aware of what is going on.' He added that he had often been mistaken for Edward VII when he was a young man and weighed sixteen stone and having researched Lillie Langtry in her native

Jersey (she was born at St Saviour's Rectory, the daughter of the rector) he felt well-equipped to talk to her if she manifested at a seance but Mrs Hamilton-Howard was not sure about the wisdom of holding a seance in the property. The original idea was to hold the seance in the room containing Edward's carved chair, which is still preserved at the hotel.

In fact the hotel is full of reminders of the royal romance including a large portrait of the Prince of Wales looking down on the dining room; and the tiles that Lillie painted are still in her bedroom.

In March 1993 I heard from Mrs Pamela Hamilton-Howard and she said: 'I must admit that personally I have not encountered a ghost at Langtry Manor – I can only say that the house has the most wonderful warm spirit evident as soon as you walk in the door … however the chef we had back in 1977-79 (Mike Weatherly) did say that at teatime he was several times aware of a grey shadowy figure floating through the kitchen and she has been seen by different guests in Lillie's apartment …'

Fifty years after she died the ghost of Lillie Langtry, a popular actress and a great beauty, caused quite a stir at the love nest she shared with Edward VII – and those sufficiently sensitive may well hear or see or sense Jersey Lily to this day.

* * * * *

Where three counties meet
Bowerchalke, Wiltshire

HERE there are numerous stories of ghosts and legends, some relevant to the fact that the village is situated where three counties meet: Wiltshire, Dorset and Hampshire. At the crossroads, a local girl who committed suicide was buried. An avenue of trees leads to the spot and it is said that birds are rarely heard singing there. She drowned herself in a well near the churchyard which is itself haunted by a procession of ghost monks who have been seen on a surprisingly high number of occasions, usually in the very early hours.

A dip in the hills nearby used to hide a curiously-shaped bush, resembling a garden seat. It was long known as Shepherd's Bush. On dark nights the ghost of a shepherd who perished here one winter's night, has been heard crying: 'I'm lost, I want to go home …' Within living memory searches have been carried out following reports of the voice being heard. Occasionally the figure of a distraught man, dressed in out-of-date shepherd's clothes, has been seen in the vicinity of the seat-like thorn bush; a figure that invariably vanishes into or near the bush.

Another valley between two hills hereabouts is also haunted. Known locally as Patty's Bottom, the valley at Woodmanton is said to have been the scene of a great battle between the Romans and the ancient Britons. Legend says the valley was filled with blood after the battle and on moonlit nights the sounds of tramping feet, frightened horses and frantic fighting have been heard.

At the east end of the village, legend has it that gold treasure is hidden in the area of Apple-spill bridge. For years on certain unspecified nights the ghost of a man carrying a lantern was reportedly seen. He seemed to follow pedestrians for a time within a limited area, rattling coins in a bag. It was thought that anyone brave enough to follow the mysterious and frightening figure would discover the treasure, but no one ever seems to have done so.

Another ghost concerned with treasure haunts the nearby downs where an ancient legend tells of a golden coffin having been hidden. On autumn nights the ghosts of seven shadowy men have

■ ... *a procession of ghost monks.*

been seen dragging the coffin over the downs.

A large house in Verne Ditch was the scene of a murder many years ago, the owner being beheaded. Very little now remains of the house, called The Lodge, but the site is reputedly haunted at nights by the sound of three distinct chopping sounds, supposed to be the sound of the head of the murdered man being chopped off.

Caught on camera
Bradford-on-Avon, Wiltshire

IN December 1992 Mrs Mildred A Carter of Gaithersburg, USA wrote to me to say that during a visit to England in October 1992, a peculiar white shape was recorded on cameras, still and video, during a visit to the Saxon church at Bradford-on-Avon.

The church of St Lawrence has been the scene of several unexplained reports of ghostly activity. Some years ago a clergyman, taking part in a communion service, saw a line of people waiting to receive communion – but they were all clothed in the dress of the 15th or 16th century. And another clergyman, in the church on a different occasion, glimpsed for a moment what he took to be a leper colony; a frightening sight that he never forgot. There was also the occasion when a visitor walked into the church which she took to be deserted and then she saw two clergymen apparently conversing very quietly, almost like conspirators, at the far end of the church. Not wishing to disturb them suddenly by her presence, she walked nearer, hearing no sound from the two who still seemed to be whispering; then she noticed that their apparel looked strangely out of date, almost from another age but before she had time to notice more the couple suddenly vanished. She never did speak to them but she searched and searched inside the church; it was completely deserted and anyway, she said no one could have possibly been there one moment and gone the next, as were the two clergymen she saw quite distinctly for a few seconds.

There were six people in Mrs Carter's party when they visited the church, once a charnel house, and none of them saw the white shape caught by the camera of Mrs Carter's father, John K Pearce of Ottawa, Canada; and he has been good enough to allow me to reproduce his picture here. The shape is also recorded on Mr Pearce's video camera (for two minutes) and on Mrs Carter's sister-in-law's 35mm camera – but it was *not* visible to the naked eye!

In the video Mrs Carter's mother is shown standing quite near the shape and then she walks towards her husband, disappearing from sight as she goes through the shape; all that is seen are her legs until she reappears coming out of the shape. At no time does the shape itself move.

Mrs Carter points out for me that it was not a sunny day; there are no windows convenient to form the shape and it cannot but be interesting that the shape was recorded by three different cameras (Mr Pearce's 35mm camera and his VHS(c) video and also the 35mm camera belonging to Mrs Carter's sister-in-law). Yet nothing was visible to anyone present!

I am exceedingly grateful to Mrs Carter who has supplied me with all possible information including the fact that the photographs were taken on 10 October 1992 around 2pm; the 'shape' does not change size or move; the whole room was in shade and the only odd sensation experienced by anyone was that Mrs Carter's mother, just after they left the church, said she was feeling very cold and she just couldn't seem to warm up. The day was on the chilly side but up to that point she had felt warm enough, as had everyone else, throughout the visit to the church. In fact it wasn't until much later that evening, after a hot bath and a cup of tea, that she really felt warm again.

A cottage near Holy Trinity church at Bradford-on-Avon has been the scene of a number of inexplicable incidents over the years. One old lady has recalled living at the cottage with her parents and sister when she was a girl and one night her sister heard strange noises which seemed to originate from the room she was occupying; noises that she likened to someone jingling with coins.

When she looked round to see whether there was any reason for the odd sounds she saw, quite clearly, the form of a man. A moment later nothing was visible. After that her sister, a calm and unimaginative sort of person, who thought she must have been dreaming, actually saw the figure on two or three subsequent occasions before the family left the cottage and moved to another house.

The girl was never really frightened; she always said the ghost did not appear to have any evil intentions towards her and she was not particularly alarmed, more interested really, but she told her sister whenever she saw the figure and, knowing her, it was accepted in the family that the girl did indeed see a ghost in the house on several occasions.

Interestingly enough a later tenant of the cottage also saw the

▓ *The strange white shape caught on three different cameras – yet not visible to the naked eye – that appeared in the Saxon church of St Lawrence, Bradford-on-Avon in October, 1992 (Photo: John K Pearce, Ottawa, Canada.)*

same ghost (or what would appear to have been the same ghost) in the same room and he knew nothing of a figure having been seen there previously. He *was* frightened and moved his bed downstairs and never slept in the 'haunted' bedroom again.

Some years later, when the 17th century cottage was being restored and modernised, part of the skeleton of a man was unearthed beneath the old flagstone floor.

✳   ✳   ✳   ✳   ✳

The haunted cottage
Branscombe, Devon

IN JULY 1992 Lynne Patterson was kind enough to write to me about a haunted cottage called Margells which was said to have once belonged to a college of friars which existed in this south Devon village. Lynne Patterson's mother, now Mrs Pardoe, was evacuated there during the Hitler war and all sorts of noises were heard then and the phantom figure of a monk was seen on several occasions.

The house, dating from medieval times, was later sold to the Landmark Trust (0628 825925) which has restored and thoroughly modernised the cottage and now rents it out for holidays and I am told that Mrs Pardoe and Lynne's sister stayed there quite recently and not only heard all manner of strange sounds but also seem to have actually communicated with the ghost monk. Before this experience, it should be noted, Mrs Pardoe was sceptical of ghostly happenings and now she is completely convinced that such things are indeed possible.

The cottage, or house, is situated near the *Fountain's Head* public house on the west outskirts of Branscombe. It once belonged to an abbey estate and probably acted as a retreat house. It is what is known as a cross passage house with the kitchen situated on the left of the entrance and the bathroom leading off; there is also a large front bedroom, a large rear bedroom and a tiny bedroom in the middle.

A small passage, now blocked up, would once have led next door to another cottage of similar age, probably 13th century, and now inhabited by two quiet elderly ladies, who also hear noises they are unable to explain; in particular a very loud banging sound which they find totally baffling.

One of these ladies experienced such an oppressive atmosphere in her bedroom that she invariably sleeps with her sister. There are no other near neighbours. The sitting room at Margells has a wonderful coffered ceiling and there are wall frescoes. Before the Landmark Trust bought the property a 'trapdoor' divided the house in two and this would regularly refuse to open for no apparent reason.

In spite of her experiences during the war Lynne's mother did not believe in the existence of ghosts, having never had supernatural experiences elsewhere, but she wanted a holiday and remembering Margells, she arranged to rent the property for a week. She took her sister with her. I now quote from Lynne Patterson's most interesting letter.

'On the night of their arrival they were washing up at 2am and standing closely together talking when suddenly a loud swishing thing moved between them at ear height. No explanation at all was found and neither my mother nor her sister had ever heard anything similar, before or since; but she had the distinct feeling that the experience was deliberate. After that, several times a day, footsteps sounded up and down the stairs and sometimes across the room upstairs; and always with the same heavy tread. Once again there was a loud crash in the kitchen while my mother was in there and this again was an unfamiliar sound but she likens it to someone shooting at a tin bread bin. Other happenings include the street door knocker sounding at 1am when no-one was around to have been responsible and there was no wind that might have caused it.

'One bedroom floor would also tap-tap-tap, as if someone was tapping on it, all night sometimes and practically every night for a while. It seemed to stop in response to light, either electric or at dawn. Most remarkable, my mother got so irritated by this that on

Margells, Branscombe, haunted by a ghost monk. (Photo: The Landmark Trust.)

her last night there she shouted, 'If you stop that we'll go away in the morning and never come back' and it was quiet all night! The last thing my mother heard was the sound of talking and chatting downstairs followed by peals of laughter. She describes this as sounding just like tuning into a distant and remote radio station while looking for another programme.

'The former tenant, who is now a successful businessman in Sidmouth, says he has heard all these things and more. He talks about the door I have already mentioned which refused to open; things being moved in that area of the house; a monk was also seen coming down the stairs of the house by the man then living there: when confronted he vanished. One of the occupants of the house was an elderly lady who died while living there. A few days before her death a white dove perched on the windowsill and stayed there until the woman died. In a specific area of the little bedroom practically every night low chanting can be heard, such as a monk saying his rosary. My mother says this room had a most oppressive atmosphere and she hardly ever went in there.

'The house is well known in the village for its hauntings but the Landmark Trust (to whom my mother has written) deny all knowledge of it. Their visitors' book does report strange noises and one young girl reports having seen a man with a bandage round his head coming downstairs.

'Although, as I have said, my mother visited the house as a girl, she never believed in the supernatural and was convinced that a rational reason would be found for the occurrences. However, since the holiday, without being unduly frightened, she is convinced otherwise now. She says that apart from the little bedroom which has an atmosphere she describes as horrible, she and her sister found the house fairly peaceful. She feels that the ghostly occupants just want to be left alone.'

* * * * *

Man in a dressing gown
Cholderton, Wiltshire

LADY Burnett-Stuart is on record as having recounted at a meeting of the Ghost Club several hauntings associated with this village on the Wiltshire-Hampshire border. As Lady Burnett-Stuart put it: 'Cholderton, like every self-respecting old village, has its ghosts.'

Cholderton House itself was long said to have the ghost of an elderly gentleman who tap-tapped his way down a narrow old staircase wearing a distinctive flowered dressing-gown. The sounds were heard by many people, residents, friends and visitors who had no previous knowledge of the reputed haunting.

The ghost is supposed to be that of a previous owner who was drowned in a well in the garden; a learned canon, no less, who met his death in 1896 but whether by accident or design has never been finally established. It is said that his bedroom slippers were found neatly arranged on the top of the well so it is hard to presuppose an accident. Lady Burnett-Stuart thought that after his impulsive and fatal action he may have regretted what he had done and returned as a warning to later occupants of his former home.

That evening the Ghost Club also heard about the haunted clump of ancient yew trees, close to Cholderton House, that is known as Yew Grove. This cluster of trees, according to tradition, was one of the sacred groves used by the Druids, possibly for sacrificial purposes. The tall and dark trees can have a frightening atmosphere of doom and sadness, even on the brightest day, and for years the place was shunned by villagers after dark.

That there are Druidic connections with the village seems indisputable. There is within the parish borders a sarsen stone, in a gully known as Devil's Ditch, which is supposed to be in some way connected with Stonehenge. The downs above the village show distinct traces of having been Celtic fields and on Quarley Hill there are traces of an Iron Age camp which may have been used by the Romans for this was part of their Post Way, the Roman road leading from Old Sarum to Silchester.

Wilbury House, in an adjoining parish, had a similar reputation to Cholderton House and local people shunned the place after darkness fell. Here, too, a phantom clergyman used to be seen, usually between the house and the lodge gates. A ghostly black retriever dog was also seen here from time to time, apparently keeping company with human beings who ventured there. Lady Burnett-Stuart revealed that she had herself spoken to four responsible people who claimed to have seen both apparitions near Wilbury House.

Here, too, a ghostly black retriever dog was seen from time to time.

In the graveyard
Combe Down, Avon

IN May 1992 Mrs Pearl Phillip was kind enough to tell me about several odd experiences she had encountered in the vicinity of Combe Down.

Among the graves of the Union Chapel, Combe Down, there is a grave dating from about 1900. One Saturday morning Mrs Phillip was walking past when she noticed a man in the labouring clothes of years gone by, at work in the graveyard with a pickaxe. Even at the time she realized with a start that what she was seeing might be an apparition but she hastened on and did her shopping.

When she returned all was quiet, the graveyard was deserted and there was no sign of any new grave or any work going on; instead bulbs and spring flowers decorated the peaceful and undisturbed graveyard.

The following Friday, at about the same time, Mrs Phillip was again passing the same way and again she saw the mysterious labourer. This time she was at the road junction, waiting to get into the traffic, when she saw the unmistakable figure. He was on the brow of the hill, just as on the previous occasion. This time she was determined to see what he was doing and she kept a careful eye on him as far as she could, bearing in mind that she was driving at the time.

Suddenly she felt very apprehensive: and then in a flash he was almost beside her, on her offside. She still kept an eye on him and noticed in particular that he was now riding a large, out-of-date bicycle. At this point there was no way he could get out of her line of sight yet one moment he was there and the next he had completely vanished.

Mrs Phillip wonders whether the man died at that spot on the road, a dangerous place where a number of people have been killed in road accidents, and whether he was buried in the nearby graveyard; or perhaps he was visiting the grave of a loved one ...

Mrs Phillip saw another ghost several times a week for nearly eighteen months in a country lane in the vicinity of Combe Down. The figure looked quite ordinary and wore a mackintosh and a

■ *The grave at Combe Down, Avon, where Mrs Pearl Phillip saw a phantom grave-digger. (Photo: Pearl Phillip.)*

beret and she invariably carried a canvas hold-all. After she had seen the 'woman' a number of times Mrs Phillip used to bid her 'good morning' or 'good afternoon' but she never received any answer and the apparently solid and real figure showed no sign of having heard the greetings.

Then one morning when she saw the familiar figure approaching Mrs Phillip thought to herself, this time she would have a really good look at the uncommunicative woman she had seen so many times, when suddenly there was nobody there; she had completely vanished in the blink of an eye! And Mrs Phillip never saw her again.

On one side of the lane, where she always saw the ghostly lady, there is a deep quarry with thick brambles on the perimeter while on the other side there is a field. Mrs Phillip wonders whether the mysterious lady met her death by accident in the quarry – or perhaps she was attacked thereabouts? On thinking back Mrs Phillip realized that it should have seemed odd to her at the time because the woman always wore the same clothes.

These are among Mrs Pearl Phillip's fascinating experiences in and around Combe Down, once the home of Ralph Allen, one of the creators of Georgian Bath.

＊　＊　＊　＊　＊

The blue fire
Coulston, Wiltshire

Baynton House here was for three years between 1852 and 1855 the home of the singular family of Samuel Savill Kent whose son by his second wife, former 'domestic governess' to the original five Kent children, was murdered in mysterious circumstances; an event that became the sensation of England in 1860 and has remained one of the most compelling unsolved murder mysteries ever known.

Bernard Taylor, author of *Cruelly Murdered* (London 1979), the most recent of three volumes devoted exclusively to the case, refers to the times when young Constance Kent, who became aware of the situation between her father and the attractive young governess while her neglected mother suffered, was not infrequently punished for bad behaviour by being shut up in one of two spare rooms at the end of a vestibule shut off by double doors – rooms that had a legend attached to them and were said to be haunted. On a certain date, once a year, a blue fire burned in the fireplace. Constance was charged with the murder.

I asked the present occupants of Baynton House whether they had any knowledge of the legend or had had any experiences that might be associated with it, for I did not recollect ever having heard a similar story, but Mrs P.A. Neaverson, the secretary at Baynton House, told me in a letter dated April 2 1993 that they had no knowledge of the legend or any ghostly activity but 'if something does come to light at a future date' they promised to let me know.

✳   ✳   ✳   ✳   ✳

The Grey Lady
Crewkerne, Somerset

IN 1986 a visitor to *The Old Parsonage Hotel* at Crewkerne related a remarkable story of a ghostly 'Grey Lady' who swanned about the bar ... and many people believed the story.

As its name implies, the building was originally the parsonage to the town's 15th century church with its long-rumoured secret passage between the two. Extensive alterations were carried out in the 18th century including a completely new front. During the intervening years the property became a farm with two nearby cottages that may well have been built over the elusive secret tunnel. A loose flagstone in one of the cottages suggests a possible entrance, although one elderly resident of the town always asserted that as a child he recalled seeing the entrance to the secret passage in one of the nearby barns – it was uncovered during renovation by workmen and when the work was completed, the entrance was filled in.

Mrs Winifred Grant and her husband stayed at the hotel in 1984 and at that time they talked with several local people who knew all about the ghostly 'Grey Lady'. They learned from the proprietors of the day, John and Therise Bolt, that there had been two sightings of the ghost within the previous twelve months; one in the hotel bar by a man who was a complete stranger to the district, in the hotel only a matter of moments. He was adamant that he had seen a white or grey shape, possibly that of a lady, which appeared and disappeared quite inexplicably.

A couple of years earlier, in the summer of 1982, Mr and Mrs William Bennett stayed at *The Old Parsonage* and they too saw 'a whitish hazy light' that appeared through the wall in the corner of their bedroom. As it moved out into the centre of the room it took the form of a woman and Betty Bennett said afterwards: 'It was clearly the shape of a woman and whilst I stared at her she vanished right before my eyes!'

Jeffrey Smithson is another witness to the unidentified White or Grey Lady. He was in the bar of the *Old Parsonage* when suddenly he saw it: an indistinct figure in the shape of a woman. 'She was sort of greyish-white and had a hazy look,' he said. 'She seemed to float over the ground and she glided towards me and then turned and disappeared before my eyes. It was a ghost all right.' Nobody knows the identity of the Grey Lady or the story associated with the ghost – or if they do they are not talking.

During the last war American soldiers were billeted in the house and there were many stories of ghost sightings then, fifty years ago. It cannot but be interesting that a similar shape, figure or form, has been repeatedly seen by different people in different parts of the house over a long period. In April 1993 I was told that *The Old Parsonage Hotel* had closed – but I am sure that had nothing to do with the mysterious Grey Lady …

☐ *The picture of Morton House in Frome, taken to show the floral display but depicting a shadowy figure resembling a swerving dispatch rider. The photograph was taken in July 1990, 50 years after a dispatch rider was killed at this spot. (Photo: Reg Wickens.)*

The dispatch rider
Frome, Somerset

IN July 1990 Mr Reg Wickens took a photograph of the floral display at Morton House on Rossiters Hill, Frome, and when the photograph was developed and printed there was the form of what appeared to be a dispatch rider on a motorcycle swerving towards the photographer. It is a photograph that has puzzled Reg Wickens ever since; especially when he discovered that a dispatch rider was killed at that spot soon after Dunkirk ... but Reg Wickens has been kind enough to let me have full details and permitted me to reproduce the puzzling photograph, so we will let him tell the story himself. This account is a combination of the experiences, investigations and reports that he has put to paper.

Reg Wickens was born during a German Zeppelin raid on Ashford, Kent, in February 1915; in fact all his family and relatives live in eastern England and he had no knowledge whatever, when he and his wife moved to Frome in the 1970s, of any ghostly happenings in the medieval town.

At first Mr and Mrs Wickens occupied a pensioners' flat in The Butts, later moving to nearby Water Lane, and each week they would go to the local sub-post office to draw their pensions, passing as they did, Morton House Guest House where they often admired the floral displays. They were especially impressed by such a display in 1990 and one lovely Sunday morning Reg decided to take some photographs.

First he took several close-up photographs of individual displays of the summer flowers and then he moved across the road to take a combined picture of the whole display at Morton House, which he did without any premonition that he was about to take a very puzzling photograph. When the colour film was completed he sent it away to be developed and printed and when it was returned from the laboratory and he was looking through the prints, he came across one which had a sticker on it suggesting that that particular print seemed to be spoiled by double-exposure; a finger over the lens; or something of the sort. But the film was used in a modern compact camera (Halina 150) where double-exposure is impossible.

Reg looked more closely at the photograph and was astonished to see that the inexplicable shadowy form depicted resembled a swerving motorcycle, apparently driven by a man dressed like an army dispatch rider, racing towards him. He noticed that the right-hand side of the photograph was normal and the whole front of Morton House was clearly visible but on the left-hand side the building is only visible through the shadowy form.

Reg looked closer still at the photograph and decided that he could distinguish a leather helmet, goggles and a long black rain-coat, which was the dress for dispatch riders in the war years. He could even make out the shape of the rider's nose and mouth. A friend looked at the photograph without being told anything and he said, 'I can't understand you standing there with a motorcycle coming towards you ...' Of course Reg saw no motorcycle. He tells me he had no special feelings when he took the photograph; he didn't notice any sensation of coldness or anything unusual although looking back he did recall the sensation that something seemed to be urging him to cross the road.

Returning to the spot where he took the photograph Reg discovered he could establish exactly where he was when he took the picture for he had stood on a manhole cover in the pavement. Wondering whether he had caught the ghost of an actual dispatch rider killed at the spot some fifty years earlier, he realized that, had a motorcyclist been in the position shown in the photograph, he must have crashed and hit the high wall at the side of the road. Later Reg Wickens learned that the place was an infamous accident black spot.

After taking the photograph, Reg learned that Field Marshal Montgomery had his headquarters at the Portway Hotel in Frome after Dunkirk and there is a metal plaque on the wall of the estab-lishment stating that Monty's divisional headquarters were estab-lished there from June 1940 and there he prepared for the vital success of El-Alamein in 1942, and acknowledging his enormous contributions to final victory. During these years he must have received many urgent messages by special dispatch rider.

Reg decided to make enquiries and he soon learned from Graham Sturgess, a retired postman, that there had been an acci-dent at Rossiters Hill during the last war, an accident in which three dispatch riders were killed. 'One of them swerved and went into the wall opposite what is now the Morton House Guest House,' Mr Sturgess said, adding: 'There was no speed limit then and no traffic lights at the junction. Those soldiers went hell for leather on their motorcycles ...' He feels inclined to accept that Reg Wickens photograph depicts one of the young soldiers killed in that accident.

Making further enquiries Reg Wickens learned that Bombardier

Thomas Gladdis of the Royal Artillery had been a dispatch rider and had been killed in a horrific crash in Frome in July 1940. His younger brother was billeted at the time in the *Vine Tree* public house and other troops were billeted in shops and houses on Rossiters Hill when the dispatch rider swerved and hit the high wall.

The obvious explanation for the figure depicted on the photograph is that it is the shadow of the photographer but this seems to be impossible. The photograph was taken at 11.30 in the morning when the sun was practically directly overhead, actually just behind Reg Wickens. There could only have been a short shadow on the pavement at that time, if any; and there could not possibly have been such a shadow as that depicted on the photograph. In any case other shots of the floral display taken immediately before and after this one, are perfectly normal without any shadowy figure.

Tolver, Gulval: The Missing Woman photograph.

The missing woman
Gulval, near Penzance, Cornwall

IN March 1993 I examined, thanks to the kindness of Michael Williams and Charles Noy (a well-known Cornish cricketer and recently retired farmer) a very curious hand-coloured early photograph.

The Noys are a pure Cornish family of great antiquity, records of the family going back to 1540. Among the celebrated members of the family is William Noy, an important Member of Parliament in the days of Charles I. In 1637 this William Noy, in his capacity as Attorney-General, imposed the controversial 'ship-money', a measure opposed by the acknowledged leader of the opposition to Charles I in the Commons, John Hampden; a man who took an active part in organising the parliamentary army in the resulting Civil War of 1642-49.

At first glance the picture seems to be a perfectly natural and normal country photograph depicting the father of Charles, Harry Noy, with two working horses and a small boy, standing in front of the family home, 'Tolver' at Gulval. But the odd thing is that two photographs were taken at the time and both by an experienced press photographer on one of the national newspapers.

In one photograph Mrs Noy, mother of the farmer Harry, stood in the doorway of the farm house and in the second photograph she stood by the garden gate. When the pictures were developed and printed Mrs Noy appeared in neither! There was merely an indistinct white patch where she had been standing waiting for the photographer; otherwise both photographs are perfect – and an even odder thing is that Mrs Noy, at the time the photographs were taken, seemingly sound in body and mind, died very suddenly afterwards.

The Quiet Woman, Halstock, near Yeovil. (Photo: Elizabeth Draper.)

The quiet woman

Halstock, Dorset

I CAME across a very unusual inn sign a few years ago at Halstock; an inn sign that intrigued me and my time was not wasted for I discovered that *The Quiet Woman* – the sign depicts a headless woman with her head under her arm – is also haunted.

The singular name and the arresting sign may owe its origin to the warped wit of some local misogynist but it is more likely to be based on the factual martyrdom of St Juthware (also known as Judware and Judith), a sixth-century woman of devout and pious disposition who was beheaded by her stepbrother for befriending early Christian pilgrims. In fact the gentle care and solitude she showed the weary and persecuted wanderers earned her the title of The Quiet Woman.

In a largely pagan Britain, Juthware's behaviour in this respect incensed her stepbrother, a staunch adherent of the old faith, and during a violent argument one day she was attacked by her step-mother and stepbrother and the latter provoked to uncontrollable rage, drew his sword and struck off Juthware's head.

Legend has it that the body of Juthware or Judith Ware miracu-lously arose and gently picking up her severed head, carried it under her arm to the chapel of St Michael at Halstock and there offered the head at the altar.

This murderous act and its aftermath is perpetuated in the unusual name of the inn, which is of much older foundation than its mid-nineteenth-century appearance implies, and in the phan-tom form of the Quiet Woman which has reputedly been dimly glimpsed on numerous occasions crossing the road at a spot about half-a-mile north of the church to a field still known as 'Judith's Field', presumably the site of her martyrdom. There have also been reports of a ghostly head which is said to have been seen in the same place.

At the inn itself there have also been occasional stories of the inexplicable appearance of a 'quiet woman'; more a shadowy figure really, almost without form, that disappears almost as soon as it has registered its appearance.

Presence of a princess
Helland Bridge, Cornwall

Delightful and comfortable *Tredethy Country Hotel* was once a royal residence; it was once occupied by Prince and Princess Chula Chakrabongse of Thailand. The Prince's cousin Prince Bira was a well-known racing motorist and I recall seeing him speeding round the haunted Brooklands race track at Weybridge.

Prince and Princess Chula loved Tredethy and today something of this romantic and popular couple still lingers among the trees and shrubs overlooking the Camel valley and especially in the house where the Prince's bedroom seems particularly infused with his presence.

Beryl Graham, who runs Tredethy with her husband Richard, has had distinct feelings in that bedroom at the front of the house and believes that if the house is haunted, it is by friendly spirits. I can confirm that, and personally I felt an overwhelming sense of the presence of the charming royal couple the first time I entered the elegant entrance porch.

I also felt the stairway to be interesting from a psychic point of view and learned afterwards that, as with so many haunted houses, the stairway is reputedly haunted: the figure of an old butler from long ago still moves silently about this house so full of atmosphere. He has been seen on many occasions to emerge from the old gun room and climb the staircase erected in 1868, so he must surely belong to an earlier date and precede the Chulas.

I understand that a ghostly lady has also been seen on the staircase landing and one cannot help wondering whether this can be Princess Chula whose ghostly form seems to have been seen hereabouts.

For ten years, from 1978 to 1988, Amanda Bristow and her family owned a cottage in this area which they visited frequently and they all spent hours walking their dogs along the old railway line and around Tredethy – a house they had heard was supposed to be haunted.

Amanda's father was with the London police all his working life and by nature, she tells me, he was not at all the sort of person to

Prince and Princess Chula photographed in 1953 with Royal Navy cadets at Tredethy, Helland Bridge.

believe such stories; his life and career were factual, sensible and down-to-earth. She feels it was fortunate that he personally experienced what he did for had it happened to anyone else he would probably have laughed at them!

One evening Amanda and her mother were entertaining a local friend, Rowena Blake, and Mr Bristow said he would leave the ladies for a chat and take a walk down the line. I now quote from the letter in which Amanda Bristow has been kind enough to describe the incident.

'When he came back his face was ashen and his lips were tightly drawn; he seemed to move slowly and carefully and we thought that he was unwell but when he had somewhat recovered he told us what had happened. "I was walking along by Donkey Pool," he said. "When I saw someone in white approaching me. They came so close that I bid them 'good evening' but they passed in front of me without saying a word and just disappeared. What struck me as much as anything was the complete silence, no crunch on the stone pebbles covering the line and no sound of movement, breaking of twigs or movement of undergrowth or bracken, nothing but silence.' "

'When he had finished Rowena Blake said at once, "You must have seen Princess Chula" and then we all talked about the stories associated with Tredethy and elsewhere but my father was unusually quiet and said very little that night or afterwards. He always seemed to find it difficult to speak of the experience, saying, "I saw something that night" and then he would momentarily drift into deep thought; it obviously made a very deep impression on him.'

If Prince and Princess Chula in another life and no longer hampered by their physical bodies find it difficult to leave the place and the area of Cornwall they loved so much, who can blame them?

✳   ✳   ✳   ✳   ✳

Back from the grave
Kentsford, near Watchet, Somerset

THE picturesque old farmhouse at Kentsford is a lasting reminder of a poignant story that goes back to the 16th-century when the property was the home of John Wyndham and his young wife Florence, whose ghostly form has been reported from time to time in Snailholt Lane and in the meadows around Kentsford.

John Wyndham was the son of Sir John Wyndham, and Florence's brother Nicholas Wadham founded Wadham College, Oxford.

In 1559 Florence fell ill and quickly became worse. Notwithstanding the frantic efforts of her husband, physicians to the family and the local apothecary, she lapsed into a coma and

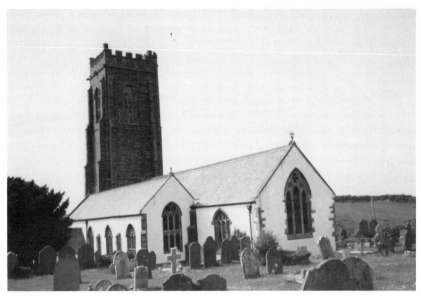

■ *St Decumen's Church, Kentsford, where Florence Wyndham was buried alive and where her ghost still walks. (Photo: W H Norman.)*

soon there was no sign of life. The cold and still body, with no detectable pulse or heart beat, was duly interred in the Wyndham family vault in St Decuman's Church.

One of those helping to place her in her coffin noticed the beautiful wedding ring she wore and a couple of nights later, unable to forget the valuable golden ring that would lie forever in the vault, this man made his way to the church at dead of night.

With only the light of a candle lantern he managed to find Florence's coffin, opened the lid without too much trouble and then found he could not prise the tight-fitting ring from the cold finger. Desperate and determined not to be thwarted, he took the knife he had brought with him and started to cut off the finger bearing the ring.

To his horror blood flowed from the jagged cut and his eyes widened still further as he saw Florence's arm slowly move ... then her eyes opened and she cried out in pain! Florence Wyndham had not died at all and her state of catalepsy had seemingly been broken by the rough treatment of the grave-robber. Like awakening from sleep she came out of her death-like trance. All this was beyond the comprehension of the wretched would-be robber and he fled as Florence slowly sat up in her coffin.

The bewildered girl soon realised her position and what had happened to her and picking up the man's discarded lantern and attired only in her burial shroud, she slowly made her way out of the vault, out of the church, down Snailholt Lane and across the meadows to Kentsford – and for years there have been numerous sightings of a white-clad female figure carrying a lantern following the same path; a figure that vanishes when it is approached.

For Florence however there was a happy ending. After recovery from the shock of her return to the land of the living she and John lived happily for many years at Kentsford where she gave birth to a son, also named John, and it is from that John Wyndham that the line continues to this day.

The old farmhouse at Kentsford; the ghostly shade of Florence Wyndham has been seen hereabouts. (Photo: W H Norman.)

Shots in the night
Langton Matravers, Dorset

VISITING authoress Rosemary Pollock at Dunshay Manor some years ago, she told us about her experiences in that beautiful manor house where she went to live with her parents, some years earlier.

'The first night we were watching television, waiting for a man to come up from the village to help us settle in. We heard the front door swing open and a voice, with a broad local accent, called out: "Is there anyone there?" Our two dogs heard him too and came with us, barking, to the door. It was open, but there was no one there.

'When the man from the village did turn up he said he hadn't been up earlier. Certainly he didn't have a broad accent. We didn't think any more of it. But it was the beginning. When she was measuring for a carpet my mother heard the most extraordinary metallic knocks. They went on for half an hour. I heard them too, later, and as I was putting a hot water bottle in the bed one night I heard a pistol shot. I was petrified. Later, other friends heard pistol shots, too.

'Things happened almost continually after that. There were footsteps on the stairs; things shook; objects moved by themselves; there were loud crashing sounds; and voices ... a psychical researcher came down but he was our only visitor who didn't see or hear anything unusual at all!

'We discovered that a previous occupant of the house had shot himself in the main bedroom, which was later divided into two rooms. We found a very ancient bloodstain on the floor under one bed.

'Even my father, who was tremendously level-headed, woke one night to find the figure of an unknown girl standing beside his bed – a girl who suddenly disappeared. We all heard the sound of a whiplash cracking in the middle of the night and most of our many visitors heard the thumpings and knockings. In the end we felt we had to leave but then, gradually, things quietened down and within months there were no disturbances of any kind. Whatever had

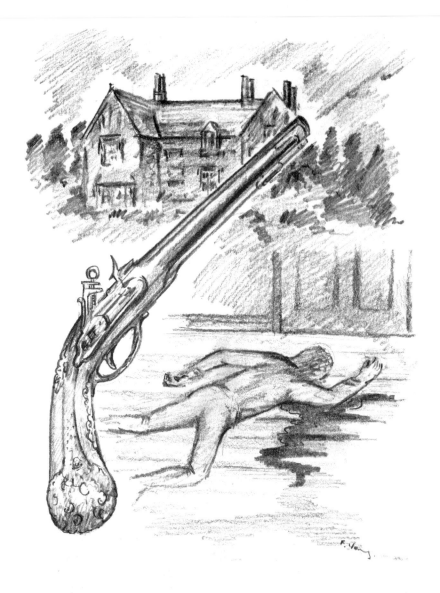

apparently objected to our presence when we moved in had become reconciled to us and we learned to love the place and live in peace there.'

46

The ghostly aviator
Larkhill, Wiltshire

THREE miles from Amesbury (where Chalk Pit Hill is haunted by the sounds of a phantom coach and horses) there is an
army camp where many servicemen have attended courses of
instruction over the years. To the north, in a small copse, there is a
stone cairn commemorating the first deaths of members of the old
Royal Flying Corps in an aeroplane accident.

Nearby, Colonel FS Cody, a pioneer of military aviation, died in his experimental aircraft. Military aviation was then in its infancy and Cody was actually the first recorded death in a powered, heavier-than-air machine. The monument however refers not to his death but to Captain B Loraine and Sergeant R Wilson, who died in 1912, the first members of the RFC to die in an aeroplane while on service.

During the second world war men of the Royal Air Force (formerly known as the Royal Flying Corps) and other servicemen were stationed at Larkhill for varying periods of time and not a few of them saw to their surprise a very small aircraft dive straight down into the wood here and disappear. Invariably the servicemen would dash to offer assistance, or call for aid, but they never found any sign of a crash or anything to account for what they had seen. On several occasions the apparition of a distinctive figure was also seen, a man in old-fashioned flying gear, usually in the vicinity of the stone cairn; a figure that invariably disappeared inexplicably, and a figure thought to be the early aviator Colonel FS Cody.

✳   ✳   ✳   ✳   ✳

A room for the night
Limington, Somerset

SOME years ago now Ghost Club members heard firsthand from Stanbury Thompson the story of the haunting of an old property he called Bramble Farm near Ilchester in Somerset.

He had just obtained his BA degree and was determined to have a nice, quiet, peaceful little break in some out-of-the-way village, with plenty of country and snug little tumbledown taverns to visit and a few scattered and picturesque farms for him to choose where he would stay.

He duly arrived in Somerset and obtained a car outside the station at which he alighted, asking to be taken to the nearest farmhouse where he would be welcomed as a paying guest. He was pleasantly surprised when the driver, a local man, told him he knew just the place, 'a big owd-fashioned house down bottom ud Bramble Lane, sir, called "Bramble Farm". Nice owd place it is. Used to be a farm, but it ain't now. Mr Frost, Frank, he wuz the only son. He left the farmin' business when his owd dad died. Methink they tek' folks in sir, providing yer want to be quiet, payin' guests, alike, to mek' a livin' … There's no family, no pets, no livestock o' any kind now, nothing – just Mister and Missus Frost lives there – just the two of 'em …'

'As darkness began to fall we drew up and driver announced that we had arrived at our destination. "If yer don't return then,' the old boy shouted after me, "I'll tek' it that yer fixed – settled – ." I turned to him and nodded.

'A quick glance at the place filled me with great delight. It was a grand old white building, half timber, with a couple of gables, and artistically graced with granite symmetrical windows, probably of a later date. Another squint furnished me with more pleasant details and particulars, and a further look convinced me that I was fully satisfied.

'Pushing open the iron gate with the toe of my boot, I swaggered up the gravelled path, or drive, to the door, plumped my two bags down and tugged at the bell. I heard it clank several times from within. Then I heard footsteps slowly approaching and I felt I was as good as settled. I signalled to my driver that all was OK, the Frosts were apparently at home; and I heard the old roadster make a sharp noise and away he sped, no doubt very pleased with himself that his suggestion had been successful. However, after waiting a few seconds for the response to my ringing, the door slowly opened and I came face to face with the person whom I took to be the Mr Frost to whom I had been recommended.

'I shivered a little at the unusual appearance of the person who stood before me: a man, tall, thin, ugly, and decrepit, and I could add, as an accurate description, a little uncouth. His face was long and drawn, his complexion, wan and sallow; he was almost a representation of death itself(!) with hollow eyes, prominent cheek bones, and grim sagging jaws.

'Yes, indeed, I thought to myself; a rare specimen of the living dead! However I was here now, my transport had gone and it was etiquette to make myself known. I found the necessary courage, with an effort, to speak and introduced myself. "Mr Frost," I stammered on rather reluctantly, "er ... I understand that you utilize this establishment of yours for the purpose of accommodating paying guests?" He nodded his head with prompt approbation, and offered his hand in a nice, kind, friendly spirit.

'Yet as I took his hand I felt a queer sensation, almost as if I had received an electric shock. That's the best explanation I am able to offer. All my nerves seemed to be on edge. I felt his long bony fingers clench my hand almost like a claw. Then I experienced a certain weakness, which came over me very suddenly; as if I was losing a great amount of vitality and I felt depressed, tired, weary and languid ... I pulled myself together a little, made known to this strange mortal my requirements and was relieved, because I now felt so very tired, when my request was approved and he humbly bid me follow him into the parlour.

'The entrance hall through which we passed, an exceptionally large one, was rather dark; somewhat long and narrow, being panelled on each side, with dark polished oak; a proper example of Jacobean craft. A curious old copper Burmese ecclesiastical lantern was suspended from the ceiling, I noticed, but this contraption gave out only a measly, half-starved light.

'The two rooms through which we passed before reaching the parlour were quite small and compact, with oaken beams, or rafters, running across the low ceilings. One must have been the dining-room and the other, most probably, the sitting-room. The walls in both the rooms were again richly panelled with dark polished oak.

'I began to realize that it was indeed an interesting, even fascinating building; well, at least, I thought, I shall appreciate the art, culture and grace of the building. As to its date; I should say it was probably about three hundred years old, an edifice, I told myself, of the Stuart period.

'It seemed too that Mr Frost had a strong liking for antiques and curiosities, for his panelling was indeed fully over-burdened with many curious fancies. He had, hanging about, weapons and old firearms of every description, and rare specimens of brass-barrelled blunderbusses, as carried by coachmen of old; wheel-lock, flint-lock, and percussion guns. I noticed too, suspended over the fire-

Stanbury Thompson, BA, who walked into a truly remarkable experience near Limington in Somerset. (Photo: The Ghost Club.)

place in both rooms, two Cromwellian helmets, with mortuary sword and breastplate to match.

'As we passed into the parlour another quantity of bygone relics attracted my attention. By the fireplace, in a recess, slowly ticking away, was an old mahogany grandfather clock. It was one of those fascinating timepieces where, fixed to the top of the dial was a kind of revolving metal plate. On the plate was painted a picture of the moon, a vivid representation, and an old-fashioned sailing boat. The moon, curiously enough, had eyes, nose and a mouth. I understand that this crude attachment to the dial was made to turn in slow revolutions, in motion with the clockwork, to depict the different actions of the moon. When normally the moon was full, the clock had worked the plate to the full extent, showing all the painted one. On the other side of the fireplace to where the clock stood, hung a pitted copper warming-pan, dated 1720, and, hanging along the side of it, a pair of blow-bellows. Gracing the mantlepiece was a pair of crudely modelled greyhounds, a small Chelsea figure, two Dresden plates, an ugly little Toby jug made by that eminent 18th century potter, Ralph Wood, and a salt-glazed bear-jug.

'Above these fancy ornaments, towering well over the fireplace was a picture, an oil-painting, in a gilded frame. It was the portrait of a lady, wearing the old-fashioned Victorian ringlets, and crude protuberant dress of the period. A Jacobean sideboard, a gate-legged table, an old Gothic stool, and two leather armchairs completed the contents of the room, apart from a few mezzotints and some neatly knitted samplers that hung on the walls. As I took all this in I noticed that my host seemed to be alone; I neither heard nor saw anyone else.

'All at once a strange condition came over me; a feeling of depression, fear, terror even; far worse than I had felt at the outside door. I felt there was something dreadfully wrong here, something unreal, something unearthly ...

'My strange host seemed to sense my dilemma and promptly made known to me his concern. "Sit down, sir, sit down ... sit down, my boy!" he coaxed quietly. "Take things easy ... relax. You'll be comfortable here. We won't disturb you."

'Immediately the *we* puzzled me. The house seemed to be deserted but for the two of us. I felt perplexed; however, the gentleman seemed courteous and obliging. Again he begged me to relax, settle myself in an armchair, perhaps close my eyes for a few moments, whilst he fried me a couple of eggs and rasher of bacon ...

■ *'I saw my host put out his hand to fondle and stroke the invisible animal; but I could see nothing.'*

'I felt somewhat languid and a good meal, and a comfortable arm-chair where I could stretch out my legs, was just what I needed and I soon did his cooking full justice. After the repast I drew my chair up to the fire, for the purpose of reading and I asked my host, out of common courtesy, if he had any objection, as I reached for my book.

'He shook his head with a dry smile. "No, of course not, sir ... Milton quoted, I believe, that a good book was the life's blood of a master spirit. Pray, my friend, you may do as you please. We won't disturb you in the least – none of us. We are very quiet, reserved, and retiring here, my wife, and our two pets."

'Before I had time to contemplate on his remark I saw the door slowly open and then close. Then I heard a heavy thud on the armchair opposite to mine, and a sigh, as if some person had sat down apparently tired and weary. Yet that person was *invisible* ... nevertheless I put it down to my exhaustion and imagination.

'Meanwhile my host settled himself down on the stool, facing the fire, leaving to my surprise, the comfortable armchair opposite to me, vacant. After a moment I found I could not settle to reading and I sat back in my chair, more than a little puzzled at the house I was in and the occupants thereof. I thought seriously of asking Mr Frost the whereabouts of his spouse – and his pets – and about the history of the house but it all seemed rather presumptuous and rather impudent. After all it was no business of mine. More than once during the next hour or so, I wished that I had chosen a more exciting, a more pleasant place for a holiday. I was already begin-ning to feel bored; my host seemed so dull and almost entirely devoid of conversation. Bramble Farm was, as I have already stat-ed, eerie, odious, and ghostly, and as night approached it seemed to me that my fears became more prevalent.

'It was now quite dark and the wind was becoming boisterous; rough and tempestuous. It almost seemed that the elements were signifying a coming storm. All at once a strange fear came over me, some preternatural feeling that strikes you that there is something wrong, something unusual, something unearthly. Some strange instinct told me that we were not alone. I was now definitely frightened, really dead scared, as the saying is. I wanted to get out. Of course that was impossible; the pitch-black night, the high roaring wind, and now rain too, put an end to that idea. Nor had I any idea where I might go. By now it was pouring with rain and I could hear it beating against the windows. The only solution, it seemed to me, was bed; not that I felt in the least sleepy but I needed relaxation of some kind and I was thinking how best to break the heavy silence when Mr Frost himself spoke.

'He called his cat. "Peter! Peter!" he ejaculated suddenly – and to my horror I heard the sound of purring coming near and nearer to us! I felt the creature's body slowly brush against me; I felt its soft sleek fur. I felt it rub its head against my leg as it passed and I saw my host stoop and put out his hand to fondle and stroke the invisible animal: but I could see nothing!

'This was enough. I hastily suggested bed. Said I was fagged out. Very tired. As a matter of fact I made innumerable excuses, so as to make it possible for me to quit these spooky surroundings then and there.

'What happened next however caused my knees to knock together, my hair to stand on end, my eyes to bulge from their sockets – for my host addressed yet another invisible inmate. He fixed his eyes on the empty chair opposite me, the same chair where I had previously heard the heavy thud. "Martha! Martha!" he said quietly, entreatingly, "Pray, go and prepare the gentleman's bed, he must be fatigued, and tired, after his strenuous day of travelling. Long journeys are indeed very tedious, very lowering."

'Adding to my terror, footsteps slowly echoed across the room at my host's request. I saw the parlour door open and then close. No doubt this invisible person had been sitting, watching me all the time. What an experience for a fellow on vacation! It was more than I could bear. There's a limit to everything, I muttered under my breath. I threw a reproachful scowl at Frost, for the ghastly ordeal he had exposed me to. I was not at all pleased; far from it in fact. Good God! to be true, the house was full of ghosts and I was helpless, more or less at their mercy … Frost seemed to have me under his full control, holding me as if in a spell. I wondered whether or not he was an arch-fiend, a sorcerer, or a wizard!

'My ruminations were interrupted as I heard footsteps of the invisible one descend the stairs, and re-open the door; her task, in all probability, had been done. The perspiration ran from me like

55

rain as the significance of all these appalling manifestations ran helter-skelter through my mind. I waited for the thing to speak: perhaps a high-pitched voice, half-devil, half-human, that would chill my blood ...

'However, old Frost turned to me and quite casually informed me that my bed was ready for me. At this juncture another invisible creature came bounding into the room, which by its panting and gasping, appeared to be quite breathless, I took to be a dog. Strange to say though, my host and I appeared to be the only mortal occupants of the parlour!

'However, I heard the dog shake its shaggy coat and I saw Frost put his hand out to pat his invisible pet, and heard him mutter some kindly expression to the animal. That was enough for me. I stammered, spluttered out impatiently, good night! And made my way as fast as I could out of the room, up the stairs and into the lighted room before me. I locked my door and made it secure by wedging a chair against it. Sleep of course was hopeless; indeed rest was equally out of the question. I turned out the light.

'I threw myself down on the bed and puzzled my brains on these strange experiences, wondering whether I had been dreaming, or imagining the gruesome visitations, or whether it was all a hallucination, or that perhaps I possessed the gift of second sight ... I lay for some little time in thought, contemplating on the whole matter when "something" sprang up, on the bed! I put out my hand, through the darkness, and came in contact with a ball of fur, and I then heard the incessant drone of purring. It was a cat – a cat! Pushing it off the bed I heard the thud, the result of its fall. The purring died away and all was quiet.

'I jumped off the bed, turned on the light, and searched the room, thoroughly, looking into every nook and corner. To my horror I was still alone; there were no traces of a cat at all. And then I heard the sounds of talking and laughing, coming from downstairs, and also the clatter of crockery and the moving of chairs. Occasionally too the barking, growling and snarling of the dog drifted up to me, adding to my distress. The incessant roaring of the wind, the pelting of heavy rain streaming wildly from the roof and down the water-spouts, added to the dismal atmosphere in which I found myself.

'However, after a while, I listened intently, trying to separate the sounds and the places they originated from; but soon fatigue overcame me and I drifted into oblivion; into a deep and sound slumber.

'The next day, as soon as I opened my eyes to morning light, there was no holding me: I was off, no hare could have moved quicker. I sprang out of bed, threw open the window, dressed myself as quickly as possible, packed my two cases, and swiftly took myself downstairs.

'I sought Mr Frost of course; to pay my reckoning, my bill, but, strange to say, he was not to be found. To my great surprise, the house was deserted – completely deserted. There was not a soul about, the whole place was as still, as silent as the tomb, and almost as uncanny.

'Anyhow I had had enough. I was not very partial to supernatural phenomena. I soon made myself scarce. I was soon outside the house and making for the gate; cursing the old cabman under my breath for my short stay.

'However, I had no sooner reached the gate when a grey-coloured sports car pulled up and the two occupants, prosperous-looking, a man and a lady, whom I took to be man and wife, sprang out and the man confronted me. He seemed rather impatient and perturbed. "Your business, sir?" he demanded, somewhat rudely I thought. "What are you doing here? Who are you?"

' "What am I doing here!" I snapped, rather embarrassed at the cold reception I had received. "Sir, my precipitated retreat should not give you a very favourable account of your miserable old dump. It is most provoking, most preposterous" I thundered; "It is quite outrageous for a professor to come for a holiday and be scared to death by a house full of phantoms."

'At this startling confession the exasperated gentleman opened his mouth wide in surprise. He swallowed and calmed down a little and seemed prepared to listen to what I had to say. And so I explained something of the ordeal I had experienced on the previous day and night; in fact I told him everything that had happened.

'Being perplexed and even it seemed a little alarmed at what I had to say, he invited me to once more enter the farmhouse,and out of sympathy for the discomfort I had received, he said, he kindly and generously offered me his hospitality. Now on better terms we exchanged compliments and he introduced himself: he was Mr Frost.

'This young Mr Frost was a charming fellow. He was well spoken, well read and very versatile. Mrs Frost was equally as gracious and just as obliging. The good lady laid out a tempting and palatable breakfast and after we had all partaken of the meal, we seriously considered with reasoned judgment the fact of my strange encounter with the unseen.

'According to Mr Frost, his father and mother had died there. They were fond of animals and in particular had two pets, a sheep dog named Lassie and Peter, a tabby tom cat. Old farmer Frost, I was told, was an enthusiastic collector of bygone relics; in fact everything fell into place. The young Frosts were so charming and keen to make up for my strange encounter that they insisted I remain to enjoy my holiday with them, as their guest, and I did so. In fact I thoroughly enjoyed the rest of my vacation; my hosts were jolly good people and did everything they could to make my stay a memorable one. Luckily too, I did not see or hear any more ghosts.

'When I got home I made one or two enquiries regarding my strange experience and I soon had the whole thing, the whole matter, explained to me. It appears, according to spiritual phenomena, that the late Mr Frost had materialized and logically collected certain matter of substance from my body that had enabled him to appear in the flesh. That, it was explained to me, was why I felt so weak, so languid, when he had taken my hand. I never visit Somerset without recalling that strange encounter with the unknown; in fact I never visit Somerset at all if I can help it.'

■ '... *I never visit Somerset at all if I can help it.*'

Ghost dogs
Lyme Regis, Dorset

AT A meeting of the Ghost Club Stanbury Thompson related an example of a canine ghost or 'spectre-dogs' as he called them. He reminded members, according to popular belief, parapsychology divided the subject into three possible sections: 1) black dogs, which are really friends that have assumed the shape of dogs; 2) the spirits of evil persons who, as part of their punishment, have been transformed into the appearances of dogs; and 3) evil spirits that mimic the sports of men or to hunt their souls have assumed the form and habits of hounds.

In the first category Lyme Regis has a famous story about one of these canine apparitions. I quote from Stanbury Thompson's account: 'About a mile from the town stands a farmhouse which once formed part of an old mansion that was demolished in the parliamentary wars, except the small portion still existing. The sitting-room now used by the farmer, and also by his predecessors for a century or two, retains the large old-fashioned fireplace, with a fixed seat on each side under the capacious chimney.

'Many years ago, when the then master of the house, as was his custom after the daily toils were over, used to settle himself on one of these snug seats in the chimney corner, a large black dog as regularly took possession of the opposite one. This dog in all essentials resembled the spectre-dog already described. For many nights, weeks and months this mysterious visitor, sitting *vis a vis* to the farmer, cast a gloom over his evening enjoyment. At length, as he received no harm from his companion, and became accustomed to his appearance, he began to look on him as one of the family circle. His neighbours, however, often advised him to drive away the fiend-like intruder; but the farmer, not relishing a contest with him, jestingly replied: "Why should I? He costs me nothing, he eats nothing, he drinks nothing, he interferes with no one. He is the quietest and frugalest creature in the house."

'One night, however, the farmer, having been drinking too freely with a neighbour, and excited by his taunts about the black dog to an unusual degree of irritation, was determined his courage should

■ '*A large black dog regularly took possession of the opposite chimney corner.*'

Lyme Regis, photographed by Ray Bishop, on a beautiful spring morning. Nothing strange or mysterious – yet the Dorset town has seen a number of manifestations.

no more be called in question. Returning home in a rage, he no sooner saw the dog in his usual place than, seizing the poker, he rushed towards his mysterious companion. The dog, perceiving his intention, sprang from its seat and ran upstairs, followed by the infuriated farmer. The dog fled into an attic at the top of the house, and just as the farmer entered the room he saw it spring from the floor and disappear through the ceiling. Enraged at being thus foiled, he struck with the poker the ceiling where the dog had passed through, and down fell a small old-fashioned box, which on being opened was found to contain a large sum of gold and silver coins of Charles I's reign.

'The dog was never seen again within the house but to the present day continued at midnight to haunt a lane which leads to the house, and which has long borne the name of Dog Lane; while a small inn by the roadside still invites the passing stranger by the ominous sign of the *Black Dog*, portrayed in all his spectral fright-fulness. As late as the year 1956 a respectable, intelligent woman asserted that she herself had seen the ghost-dog.

"As I was returning to Lyme," she said at the time, "One night with my husband down Dog Lane, we had about reached the middle of the lane when I saw an animal about the size of a dog approaching us. 'What's that?' I asked my husband. 'What,' he said. 'I see nothing.' I was so frightened I could say no more, for the animal was within two or three yards of us and seemed as large as a young calf but had the appearance of a black shaggy dog with fiery eyes, just like the descriptions I had heard of the ghostly Black Dog. It passed close by me and made the air cold and dank as it passed. Though I was afraid to speak, I could not help turning round to look after the creature and I saw him seemingly swelling into a large cloud and then he vanished into the air. As soon as I could speak, I asked my husband to look at his watch, and it was then five minutes past midnight. My husband still says he saw nothing but a vapour or fog coming up from the sea."

'It might be said that a case of this kind shows how even a sensible person may become the victim of self-delusion but I would remind everyone that in all practical matters this woman was remarkably sober-minded, intelligent and judicious, and well educated for a person of her calling – that of sick nurse, the duties of which she discharged in the recorder's house for several weeks to his fullest satisfaction, showing no symptoms of nervousness or timidity or excessive imagination.'

✳   ✳   ✳   ✳   ✳

The girl in the black gloves
Melksham, Wiltshire

A HAUNTED car was reported to frequent the road here-abouts a few years ago; not a ghost car but an aged Morris whose owner Andrew Parks, encountered to his surprise, four ghosts – sometimes sitting on the bonnet and sometimes on the roof of the car.

At first there was only one ghost, a girl with long dark hair and wearing long, black gloves and little else! After the car was exorcised by a priest the ghostly girl vanished for a fortnight and then returned bringing with her three almost identical friends. The Rev. Thomas O'Donovan of St Anthony's Church, Melksham said at the time: 'Mr Parks came to see me, frightened, and asked for my help. It was a short, straightforward service, during which I asked God's protection for the car's occupants and protection for Mr Parks.'

Mr Parks reportedly said: 'I don't mind the ghosts … the four of them are exactly the same … they seem to be in black and white, not colour. Sometimes they sing to me and one of them has a guitar. They call me "Andy" but I cannot make out anything else they say or what they are singing. They have strong accents that I do not understand; possibly it is Scottish, possibly Welsh; certainly not Irish. I have tried to lip-read but I can't make out what they are saying at all …'

Interestingly enough the figures were also seen by an acquaintance who claimed mediumistic powers. He claimed to see one of the girls sitting on the car bonnet.

This road where Andrew saw his first ghostly passenger runs past an old cemetery but the connection with the apparitional girls did not occur to him; it was the priest who exorcised the car who first suggested a possible correlation.

Soon, as so often happens, these phantom forms disappeared as mysteriously as they had appeared and the roads around Melksham became as ghost-free as they always had been – as far as we know!

The haunted Morris car with its strange roof passengers.

'Suddenly I was aware that a man stood at my bedside.'

The man in the portrait
Mere, Wiltshire

A TRUE ghost story was recounted at a meeting of the Ghost Club in 1958. Forty years after the event it was still vivid and real to the percipient, a long-standing member of the Club. He said:

'On the night of 12th October 1918, I woke suddenly and saw a patch of greyish-yellow light near the window. At the time all I thought was that it presaged the dawn, whereas I wished for more sleep, but I lay awake looking at the patch of light.

'Presently I noticed that the light did not enable me to see anything in the room, nor did it increase as it should have done were it the dawn breaking. Suddenly I was aware that a man stood at my bedside. I sprang up, and drove my fist into – and *through* him!

'I fell part-way out of bed, recovered my balance with difficulty, and fell back on my pillows. I lay there gasping, conscious of the fact – the astounding fact – that I was gazing at a visitant from another world!

'The ghostly form then moved slowly towards the patch of light and was very gradually absorbed into it, the light slowly fading away until there was no figure and no light. The whole affair lasted about twenty minutes, or so it seemed to me, counting from when I first became aware of the strange light to the time when it had completely disappeared.

'Seven or eight months later I was in a house in the village and noticed a portrait across the room, a portrait that made me say to myself: "That is exactly like the ghost I saw!". I walked over and found that it was the portrait of a man who had once lived in the house I occupied, and who had died there, very suddenly.'

The evening visitor
Portland, Dorset

A FEW years ago George Marshall of Co. Antrim, told his first-hand ghost story to several people and it was published in a weekly magazine. One evening George was relaxing in front of the fire; his wife was out and Sue, their pet dog, was asleep at his feet. Suddenly he heard the click of the heavy door latch and turning he saw the door slowly open a little way.

George was puzzled. For the door to open it was necessary to work the latch and he had heard the latch, yet George knew he was alone in the house ... there wasn't a breath of wind or a draught anywhere that night.

Suddenly Sue was awake and growling. She was on her feet, facing the door, her eyes riveted at a spot that would be about the height of a person's head. As she stood there her ears flattened, her hair stood on end all along her back and her mouth was set in a savage, quivering, snarl.

George Marshall was astonished for in all the years they had had the dog he and his wife had always found her to be extremely docile, gentle and lovable. She was acting completely out of character. 'What's the matter, Sue?' he asked but she paid not the slightest attention to him and started to tremble and her eyes moved slowly along the wall, all around the room and back towards the door. All the time Sue's eyes seemed set on something invisible and unblinking and completely engrossed she followed whatever it was behind George's chair – driving her almost wild; she snarled and snapped as if to protect her master ... he saw nothing but her attitude was beginning to affect him and he felt the hair on his scalp starting to prickle.

Whatever it was apparently reached the door at last and then Sue calmed down a little, her hair began to lie down again and she stopped growling. George assumed that whatever had come into the room had now gone out again. He tried to coax the animal into the hall as he went to investigate and make sure nothing was there, but she wouldn't move. Satisfied that nothing visible was in the hall, George resumed his seat by the fire and took up his book again.

Cautiously and quietly the dog edged towards the door. She poked her nose into the hall and then walked out of sight and George heard her scratching and sniffing about before she eventually came back and lay down at his feet.

It was the only time the corgi ever acted in that way and George was reluctant to pooh-pooh the event of that evening; but he was relieved that whatever had come into the house that night had gone out again and never returned. But what was it?

A village of ghosts
Purton, Wiltshire

A VILLAGE that is first mentioned in writing in Saxon times; where Ringsbury Camp on the edge of the village was a fortified dwelling long before the time of Christ; a place known to the ancient Romans whose relics and remains have been discovered in many parts of the village - should surely be haunted and indeed it appears to be, by a variety of ghosts.

A phantom horseman has long been seen and heard on one of the roads that lead out of the village; and a nun is said to haunt Purton church, long thought to be the woman whose skeleton was found there in 1872, bricked up in a cavity of the chancel wall. But I asked the rector, the Rev Canon R.H.D. Blake whether he had had any strange experiences and he tells me in a letter dated February 12 1993: 'In nineteen years in the parish, and in and out of the church, day and night, including one or two nights spent wholly in the church, I have never seen or heard anything unusual ... however there is a mystery about the lady discovered in the wall ...'

Canon Roy Blake was kind enough to send me a copy of his *History and Guide to St Mary, Purton* wherein I learned that restoration of the church in 1872 resulted in a remarkable discovery: 'In the angle formed by the north transept and the chancel there was a room or chapel, long disused and its windows and entrances blocked up. Today it is the sacristy. Mrs Prower, widow of Major Prower, writing in 1894, says: "There was a window on the north side, filled with stones and almost hidden with ivy. A small staircase led up from the chapel to a tiny low room above, with just room perhaps for a pallet."

'This chapel, with the small room above, was known to exist behind its sealed doors and windows, but had not been entered for generations. Twenty years before it had been suggested to Canon John Mervin Prower that it might be adapted as a robing room, but he rejected the proposal and insisted that the subject should never be raised again. He said that the history of the abandoned chapel bore some reference to a former vicar and that a "dark deed" had been committed there.

'In the course of restoration the workmen opened up the old chapel. They found that its east wall was hollow, about four feet above the ground. They broke into the wall and found a body lying at full length. The head and shoulders lay in a cavity cut into the chancel wall, the rest of the body in the wall of the chapel.

'Whose was this body? Why was it there? What was the original purpose of the chapel with its little room above, and why had it been sealed up? We can only speculate.

'The Victorians thought that they had uncovered the cell of an anchoress, a female recluse. They may have been right. Male hermits or anchorites, and female anchoresses, were not uncommon in the pre-Reformation Church. They lived in a small cell which was usually attached to a church. This would have one window through which the occupant could see the altar and take part in worship, and at least one other through which the recluse was fed and from which she offered spiritual advice to visitors.

'It seems quite possible that our present sacristy might once have been the cell of an anchoress, but was it her body in the wall? Those who saw the body before it fell away into dust on exposure to the air said that it was a female figure, but why bury an anchoress in the wall? Surely, even if her life had been spent within the four walls of the cell, she would have been buried in the normal way in the churchyard? And what of Canon Prower's story of a previous incumbent's dark deed?

'A romantic and anti-Catholic Victorian writer had an entirely different idea. In a poem it is claimed that the body was that of a pre-Reformation nun, who had erred in some way, and was walled up while still alive. Adding to the mystery it is said that various objects were found by or near the body, among them a dagger with a broken blade, a sword and parchments.

'However, the workmen seem to have taken away everything that they found and we have no account of the discovery from a reliable eye witness. Twenty years later, Mr J. Elton Prower, son of Major Prower and grandson of the last Vicar Prower, tried to get at the truth and interviewed one of the workmen … He did succeed in buying back the sword for ten shillings and it is now in a glass case on the north wall of the chancel, close to the place where it was uncovered. Historians of arms tell us that the sword dates from the mid-17th century. It can have no connection with a pre-Reformation nun or anchoress. But is it connected with Canon Prower's story of a previous Vicar and his "dark deed"? It is, after all, only a century older than his father's arrival in the parish, and in the country memories live long. The mystery remains.'

'If there is a ghostly nun,' says Canon Blade in his letter to me. 'Clearly she can have no connection with the body in the wall.' But ghostly nun there does appear to be. Miss Sarah White wrote to me at the end of 1992 and I cannot do better than quote from her most interesting letter: 'I am currently reading your book, *Ghosts of Wiltshire* and I find it fascinating. I am, however, rather disappointed that you don't investigate our village, Purton. I am rather sensitive to the presence of ghosts; maybe because for the first fourteen years of my life I lived in a house with at least one ghost. There were many sightings of ghosts there, still remembered by my family, and most times it was the ghost of a man.

'The house was built in the early 1800s, I think, in the Tudor/Elizabethan style. My uncle saw a ghost dog there and one of my sisters saw the ghost of a woman. The house is semi-detached and the son of the people next door thinks that there is a ghost woman there as well. We also had friends who used to bring their children over and put them to bed upstairs. Several times someone downstairs heard what sounded like a child walking along the landing and part of the way down the stairs; then the footsteps would stop and a voice would call out, "Mum …" When a parent or anyone went to see who it was, no one was ever there. Naturally the parents would check on the children and invariably they were all in bed and fast asleep.

'The local church also has a ghost. The church dates back to the 1200s and somewhere through the ages a nun was bricked up in one of the walls. The body was discovered when there was structural alterations in the church. I have seen the nun but I didn't realise what I was seeing until I read the book about the church. I then discovered that the place where I saw her was roughly the place where she had been bricked up.'

Miss White adds: 'Our old house is now in the hands of a family whose daughter has been frightened by the ghost.' In a subsequent letter Miss White writes: 'I have now spoken to the people who

▨ *A ghostly nun appears in the church.*

The church of St Mary, Purton, with its mysterious and secret room and ghostly nun-like figure that has been seen within the last few years. (Photo: Canon R H D Blake.)

live next door to the house where we used to live and they are sure that the ghost is that of a woman; but there is also a ghostly man. On one occasion the parents went on holiday and left their son to look after the house and the cats. One day the son arrived home from work and went to call the cats for tea; suddenly he heard a double clap from immediately behind him. He turned, expecting to see his father, but there was no one there. When his father called the cats for tea he always clapped twice.

'When we lived in that house my mother awoke one night to see what she thought was my father standing at the bottom of the bed. She reached to turn the light on and the figure turned and walked towards the door. When the light was on the figure suddenly vanished.

'My uncle is psychic too. One evening when he was visiting he went into a sort of trance and said there was a man in the room; a man in Victorian dress and there was a dog by his side ...'

Miss White has been kind enough to approach several people in Purton with experiences to relate and they included Mr CR Shailes who tells me he was walking his dog down a narrow path near the church, one day in late spring, 1989, when the dog suddenly stopped in his tracks and pricked up his ears, standing stock still as he reached a bend in the path. On reaching the bend himself Mr Shailes saw three children playing in the distance. What struck Mr Shailes as odd was that the dog would usually have bounded towards the children but this time, even when patted on the head and spoken to, he was very reluctant to proceed.

Then Mr Shailes noticed something else very odd: there was no sound of movement or laughter or talking, nothing. He and the dog continued towards the children. When they were closer Mr Shailes saw that the children were all dressed in long and dark clothes and each of them had a posy of flowers in their hands. When he was about twenty yards away the children suddenly all ran off - and still there was no sound.

The path joins a road a little further on and when he reached that point Mr Shailes found there was no sign of the children: nor was there any trace of them in the two other possible directions. They seemed to have completely vanished. The children had all seemed to be around six or eight years old and the sighting took place during school hours, in term time, when children of that age would be at school.

Mr Shailes tells me he had one other odd experience on the same path. One night in the summer of 1990 he had a vivid dream in which he saw a light aircraft appearing to attempt to use the field beside the path as a landing strip. He saw the aeroplane land - and then crash in the wood on the right-hand side of the path. Later that day he walked down the path, with his dog, and stopped to watch an aeroplane landing. As he watched he realized that this was exactly what he had dreamed about and he stood and watched the aircraft land and then crash into the wood, precisely as he had dreamed. Fortunately, he learned afterwards, there was no loss of life.

Mrs Eileen J. Hunt of Reids Piece, Purton, tells me that she does not believe in ghosts; however, one afternoon she and her husband were taking their dog for a walk and on the way home they walked along Church Path ... 'and saw two youths walk out from the trees right in front of us. We followed them along the path, they were laughing and talking to each other and you could see the movement of their mouths - but we could not hear a sound. Suddenly they both walked into a bush at the side of the path and completely disappeared!'

* * * * *

The ghost that saved a child
Salisbury Plain, Wiltshire

IN 1986 a young mother, Mrs Sturgess, seems to have returned from beyond the grave to save the life of a three-year-old child after she and her own young son were killed in a horrific road accident at the same spot.

She reportedly appeared in front of the army truck being driven by her widowed husband during an army display on Salisbury Plain. Mark Sturgess, at the time a 26-year-old serving soldier, was driving between two other service vehicles when he suddenly saw his wife materialize.

He said afterwards: 'My wife was standing there as clear as day and she was wearing the same sweatshirt and jeans she had on the day she and our son died. She glided close to the front of my lorry. The hairs on the back of my neck stood up; a shiver ran down my spine; and I slammed on the brakes. As I sat there in shock a family from the audience wandered out from behind the very next truck and a three-year-old boy ran straight in front of me. If I have not seen the ghost of my wife and stopped, that boy would have undoubtedly been killed.'

No longer in the army but working as a warehouseman, Mark has never had any doubt about the form he saw. 'I could never have coped if that boy had been killed', he said later. 'After seeing my

■ *'My wife was standing there …'*

wife and son die when a car driven by a drunken driver mounted the pavement, it would have been too much … my wife has never returned again but I know she came to protect me and that little boy at a time of awful danger'.

Monks and nuns
Shaftesbury, Dorset

THE *Grosvenor Hotel* here, a Forte Heritage establishment, centuries old, has several ghosts and the manager Terry Roper has been kind enough to let me have some details.

The Saxon hilltop town of Shaftesbury was founded as a settlement by Alfred the Great in the year 888 and he built a Benedictine Abbey there for nuns, with his daughter Ethelgyra as the first Abbess. The town became a place of pilgrimage to honour the shrine of St Edward the Martyr. He had come to the throne at the age of fifteen in 975 but was murdered three years later at Corfe Castle and hurriedly buried at Wareham. A year later his body was moved to Shaftesbury, amid great excitement. He was declared a saint in 1001, with a feast day of March 18 and many miracles of healing are reputed to have taken place at his tomb.

In the 17th and 18th centuries, the *Grosvenor*, then called *The Red Lion*, was a regular stopping place for horse-drawn coaches with names like 'Quicksilver' and 'The Phoenix' that used the five turnpike roads which converged at Shaftesbury; and it may be from these heady days that one of the *Grosvenor* ghosts dates.

Although there are no written records before 1541 it is likely to be over a thousand years since travellers and pilgrims first sought rest and shelter at some primitive inn here that has grown through the centuries to become the *Grosvenor* of today.

Throughout all these years the *Grosvenor* has laid claim to a number of ghosts and a whole series of isolated incidents has left successive managements and guests puzzled about the origins and identities of the various apparitions.

In medieval times a certain Sir Osbirt Gifford was excommunicated – and possibly whipped in Shaftesbury's market place – for stealing two nuns from the Abbey. Can it be one of these stolen nuns who has been seen flitting about the hotel in recent years, a figure usually referred to as the Grey Lady? And why does a ghostly monk lurk in the shadows from time to time? Can he have anything to do with the labyrinth of ancient tunnels running under the hotel – passageways that were once regularly frequented by monks? And what are we to make of the ale often reported missing from locked and guarded cellars?

Not without cause is the *Grosvenor* at Shaftesbury included among the haunted hotels which guests and ghosts are loth to leave.

* * * * *

An explorer's experience
Somewhere in Wiltshire

IT was from John Blashford-Snell, the delightful, experienced and enterprising worldwide explorer who spends his life pushing back the frontiers of science and mysteries of all kinds, at a Ghost Club meeting, that I heard about a haunted Tudor farmhouse in Wiltshire. The exact location cannot be divulged as the property was only rented and is now occupied by a family with young children.

Colonel Blashford-Snell, MBE, had just flown in from Washington and planned to motor home to Yorkshire next day but after his eight-hour flight across the Atlantic, all he was looking for was a good night's sleep as he drove up to the Scientific Exploration Society's base in Wiltshire, at midnight. As chairman of that organisation he had arranged with his old friends Jim and Jane, the wardens of the base, to spend the night there, although they had told him they would be away that night.

He found the key left for him and entered the warm and welcoming house, switched on the light and found a note from his friends asking him to use the bathroom at the top of the stairs. As he prepared to retire he heard the sound of coughing in the room directly above him. For a moment he thought it odd and then he remembered his friend's teenage son, Michael, usually slept in the room over the kitchen. He realized that he must have woken the boy up and decided to be more quiet. Ready for bed at last he tip-toed up to his bedroom where he was soon fast asleep.

Awake with the sun, he got up, hearing as he did so Michael dressing in his room and as he bathed he saw Michael's shadow cross the frosted-glass door, followed by clumping footsteps that descended the narrow wooden stairs. As he dried himself the shad-ow of Michael passed the door again and returned to his bedroom. John Blashford-Snell called out 'Morning, Michael' but there was no reply.

Dressed and downstairs John telephoned his wife and as he did so he could hear Michael still moving about in his room. Suddenly there was the sound of a car and the outer door opened and in walked his friends Jim and Jean. 'Hallo, John – sleep well?' they asked. 'Yes – super,' John replied and they chatted for a moment and then he added, '… I'm sorry I disturbed Michael last night.'

They looked at him in a strange way. 'Michael?' they said. 'Michael has not been here for six weeks – he's away at college.' 'Then who on earth is upstairs?' John asked. 'And he's still there.'

They all went upstairs to Michael's room. The door was closed but when they went inside the room was deserted. They searched the house from top to bottom. All the doors and windows were tightly closed.

Jim and Jean then revealed that a number of mysterious happen-ings had occurred at the old farmhouse. The fact that they are two of the most practical and down-to-earth people one could meet made the story all the more remarkable.

From time to time both of them, and Michael too, had noticed strange noises, sounds of movement; and they had encountered a silver-haired lady in Michael's bedroom. Once Jim, a stolid West Country man, was alone in his workshop on the farm when the door opened by itself and he became aware of feeling suddenly cold. He turned and standing in the doorway was a man. He appeared to be completely normal, of medium height, having a ruddy complexion, about fifty, and dressed like a farmer. When Jim recovered from his surprise at seeing a stranger there, he asked: 'What are you doing here?' And the next second the 'man' had gone – quite literally he had vanished into thin air! Jim moved quickly and looked everywhere but there was no sign of the figure

■ *'He saw Michael's shadow cross the frosted-glass door.'*

he had seen.

Later John told the owner of the farm the story of the curious happenings and the apparitional man and silver-haired lady; but he knew of no previous history of haunting, no accounts of terrible deeds, nothing that might give rise to a haunting but he promised

to make enquiries.

Some months later he told John that he had discovered something interesting. A person fitting the description of the silver-haired old lady had once lived at the farm. Her husband, who had been much younger than her, had been employed on the farm some years ago and she had in fact died in that bedroom – Michael's room: where her form had been seen. But she had died from natural causes, there was no question of murder or anything; and the man, who seemed to be her husband – well, that was even odder for he was alive and well and lived about ten miles away! Needless to say he never visited the farm.

John Blashford-Snell has always thought how appropriate it is that an intriguing mystery should be associated with the one-time headquarters of an organization dedicated to solving mysteries!

*   *   *   *   *

◀ *Colonel John Blashford-Snell MBE in Tibet in 1987. He once had a remarkable psychic experience in Wiltshire. (Photo: The Scientific Exploration Society.)*

Headless horseman
Stourton, Wiltshire

BROOK House here, the dower house of Stourhead Estate, has a bricked-up window and a boarded-up room (or had a few years ago).

These drastic alterations were said to be the result of the haunting of that part of the house by the ghost of an old woman and a black dog.

Years ago a local man chose to sleep in the haunted room and the phantom form of an old woman appeared at the foot of his bed. When he shouted at her she disappeared but in the morning when he awoke all the clothing had been stripped off him and off the bed, even the bolster being removed from its case.

A headless horseman is said to haunt the Sloane Track, which leads from Penselwood to the lower end of Stourton (an area once known as Gasper), followed by a black dog.

The story goes that a man made a wager at Wincanton Market that he could ride to his home at Stourton in seven minutes flat. He took a cross-country route but the horse stumbled and threw him as he galloped down the Sloane Track. The man's neck was broken and now his ghost haunts the road, followed by his faithful black dog; but only on New Year's Eve – possibly the anniversary of the event.

* * * * *

Betsy Grimbal
Tavistock, Devon

EARLY in 1993 I first heard of the ghost, known as 'Betsy Grimbal', (a young girl, reputedly murdered by a villainous monk) that has been seen and heard by various members of the staff of the *Bedford Hotel*, Tavistock, over the years. Visitors have also had odd experiences and I am indebted to Mrs Jill Beale at the hotel for subsequent information.

It seems that several staff members have heard and felt and occasionally glimpsed the presence, especially during the early hours of the morning and especially in the vague vicinity of the reception area.

In the spring of 1993 Mrs Croft, a medium, stayed at the hotel while taking part in a film being shot on Dartmoor and she felt great unhappiness in the vicinity of the outbuildings. She thought this was connected with a stable boy of years gone by and she mentioned the date of 1734. Mrs Beale tells me a hostelry called the *Dukes Arms* was built on the site of the present *Bedford Hotel* between 1734 and 1741. The medium also had the name Howard Franklin quite clearly but Mrs Beale has been unable to find any appropriate references.

One evening Mrs Croft passed a phantom lady coming up the stairs. She described the figure as wearing a long, dark dress and a frilled bonnet. Her lips were pursed but she had a kindly look and carried a large bunch of keys; the medium thought she might be a former housekeeper.

Mr Croft encountered a phantom soldier in the residents lounge. He was wearing a First World War uniform and stood in front of the fireplace, but seemed very impatient and agitated and worried about something – but almost as soon as the visitor saw the figure, it had vanished.

On occasions the hotel's manager, John Barker, has worked late in the computer room, which is located by the reception area, and in the very early hours, between one and two in the morning, he has distinctly felt someone walk past the room. This has happened several times, although no doors have opened as would be neces-

The Bedford Hotel, Tavistock, in Edwardian times.

sary for a human being to pass that way and the fire doors are always closed at night. Mr Barker has also occasionally had the uneasy but vivid feeling that someone was watching him; and the same feeling has been experienced by another staff member in the same area.

The hotel maintenance engineer, working late one night laying carpet in the reception area, between one and four o'clock in the morning in fact, heard the rustle, as of a long dress followed by the sound of someone walking past but he saw nothing. He too has experienced the sensation of being watched, and usually in the same area.

The head chef was working late one night on the lower ground floor when he saw a lady walk past the door; she was dressed in a long, dark dress and wore a bonnet with a neck frill. The dress rustled along the corridor.

Mrs Beale tells me that all these witnesses of what may well have been manifestations of the ghost of Betsy Grimbal gave her their stories completely independently and she knows that there have been other sounds and sighting that suggest that the *Bedford Hotel* has durable ghosts and phantoms.

A gentle ghost
Wadebridge, Cornwall

I FIRST met the late and much missed James Turner, poet, author and broadcaster, when he owned the site of Borley Rectory in Essex, long known as 'the most haunted house in England'. But he lived in Cornwall for the last twenty years of his life and while there he wrote about the ghosts and haunted houses of the South West.

He and his wife Cathy were no strangers to ghosts. They had lived in a haunted and distinctly disturbing rectory at Layer Marney in Essex and at other houses regarded as haunted before they moved to Borley where they both experienced a wealth of inexplicable happenings including footsteps, bangs and crashing sounds that had no rational explanation; voices 'happy and laughing' that fled before them time and time again in the garden; strange and unexpected smells; even a phantom cat.

While writing about ghosts in the Westcountry James had a few personal experiences which he did not always reveal in his books. He loved Roughtor, the second highest tor in Cornwall (where his ashes are scattered) and always regarded it as haunted. One of the loneliest places in Cornwall, he called it, and alive with the 'spirits' of people who lived and worked and died there.

One of the cottages in Cornwall that James and Cathy lived at was Treneague, near Wadebridge, once the property of the monastery at nearby Pawton, possibly one of its out-farms. Here, within living memory, ghost monks have been seen sitting on a bench in one of the quiet, cool rooms; while another cottage, 'Lower Treneague', further down the valley, had an invisible ghost. James told me that once when he visited that cottage, the occupants suggested he might like to spend a little while along in one of the bedrooms and he was certain, ever after, that while he was in that room he suddenly felt an invisible child's cold hand placed in his. After a couple of seconds it had gone but there was no doubting the experience. Only afterwards did he learn that many people, spending a time quietly alone in that particular bedroom, have experienced the same phantom hand – perhaps that of a child who

To Peter & Joyce
with
Best wishes
from
James
14.8.62

30.1.61

■ *James Turner, poet, author and broadcaster, whose individual presence returned after his death. (Photo: Peter Underwood.)*

died there and still seeks the warmth of human comfort.

At Bettiscombe House near Bridport in Dorset James saw a haunted rocking chair gently move to and fro, and in the childrens' bedroom there he distinctly heard the sound of children laughing and talking although there had been no children living in the house for many years. But in his beloved Cornwall he saw, heard and felt more ghosts than he usually admitted to.

Many times after his death Cathy told my wife and I (we stayed with her twice a year at Wadebridge for many years) that she was often conscious of the individual presence of her dead husband. Not in any unpleasant way; it was simply that at the most unexpected times she would suddenly be aware that he was in the room with her and she would talk to him and find comfort from his presence – although she often chided him for leaving her so suddenly. He had died in his sleep without any previous warning of ill-health. A gentle, quiet man in life, he would, I am sure, be a gentle, quiet ghost.

■ *Enchanted Cornwall, a country of legends and ghosts where the past seems very near.*

The tolling bell
Wilcot, near Devizes, Wiltshire

HERE, according to Ghost Club member Mrs W Gilbert, there is a famous ghost legend, known far and wide throughout the parish and beyond.

About the year 1761, in the parish of Wilcot, in the vicar's house to be exact, there was heard for a considerable time the sound of a bell constantly tolling every night. The occasion was said to be as follows:

A debauched person who lived in the parish came one night very late and demanded the keys of the church from the vicar, that he might ring a peal. The vicar refused to let him have the keys, alleging the unreasonableness of the time, and that he should, by granting his desires, give disturbance to Sir George Wroughton and his family, whose house adjoined the churchyard. Upon this refusal, the fellow went away in a rage, threatening revenge.

Some time later this man went to Devizes and there met with one Cantle (or Cantlow) a person noted in those days for a wizard, and to him he related how the vicar had served him, making himself out to be the injured party and begging some help to get even with the vicar.

The reply Cantle made to him was this: "Does he not love ringing? He shall have enough of it!" And from that time a bell began to toll in the vicar's house, and continued to do so until Cantle's death. Before he died Cantle confessed in Fisherton Gaol, in Sarum (where he was confined by King James) that he had caused the sounds, and that they would be heard as long as he was alive.

The ringing became so famous that persons came from all parts of the country to hear it, and King James himself sent a gentleman from London on purpose to give him satisfaction concerning the truth of the reports. A certain Mr Beaumont researched the story and obtained details from Sir George Wroughton's own grandson; with an additional remarkable circumstance; that if anyone in the house put their heads out of the window they could not hear a sound, but they heard the ringing again immediately they withdrew their heads from the window and stood again in the room.

For proof of the story there are the testimonies of two divines, that of a man of quality and probity, and the satisfaction of a learned king who had sent a responsible man to inquire into the matter. After this, it has been suggested, there can be little room for doubt concerning the story accepted in the locality for over two hundred years. Mrs Gilbert ended her historical account of an historical ghost by saying that she, for one, had no doubt whatever as to the authenticity of the story.

* * * * *

ACKNOWLEDGEMENTS

The author acknowledges with gratitude the help and co-operation of his wife and the following: Revd Canon RHD Blake and his excellent *History of St Mary's Church, Purton;* Colonel John Blashford-Snell, MBE (who published his personal experiences of ghosts in his volume *Mysteries* London, 1983); Mrs Jill Beale; Amanda Bristow; Mildred A Carter of Gaithersburg, Maryland, USA; Elizabeth Draper; Mrs Pamela Hamilton-Howard; Yvonne Hearn, Bath Tourism and Marketing; Eileen J Hunt; George Marshall; Mrs Rebecca Morgan, The Landmark Trust, Shottesbrooke, Maidenhead, Berks; Mrs P.A. Neaverson; WH (Ben) Norman (author of *Legends and Folklore of Watchet,* published by the author from Lyn Cottage, Mill Lane, Watchet, Somerset, 1992); Mrs Pardoe; Miss Lynne Patterson; John K Pearce of Ottawa, Canada; Mrs Pearl Phillip; Rosemary Pollock; Terry Roper; Mr CR Shailes; Mark Sturgess; Anthony Sutherland; Miss Sarah White; Reg Wickens and especially Michael Williams for several original items and who published a fascinating piece about Tredethy, Helland Bridge, in his *Supernatural Search in Cornwall.*

By the same author
Ghosts of Cornwall
Ghosts of Devon
Ghosts of Somerset
Ghosts of Dorset
Ghosts of Wiltshire
Westcountry Hauntings
Mysterious Places
The Ghost Hunter's Guide
This Haunted Isle
Queen Victoria's Other World
Dictionary of the Supernatural
The Ghost Hunters
Haunted London
Into the Occult
Deeper into the Occult
Gazetteer of British Ghosts
Gazetteer of Scottish and Irish Ghosts
Ghosts of Wales
Hauntings: New Light on Ten Famous Cases
A Host of Hauntings
The Vampire's Bedside Companion
The Complete Book of Dowsing and Divining
Ghosts of North West England
Ghosts of Kent
A Ghost Hunter's Handbook
Ghosts of Hampshire and the Isle of Wight
Lives to Remember: A Casebook on Reincarnation (with Leonard Wilder)
The Ghosts of Borley: A critical history of
            'the most haunted house in England' (with Dr Paul Tabori)
Jack the Ripper: One Hundred Years of Mystery
Death in Hollywood
Ghostly Encounters
A Ghost Hunter's Almanac
Ghosts and How to See Them

Biography
Horror Man – The Life of Boris Karloff
Life's a Drag – A Life of Danny la Rue

As Editor
Thirteen Famous Ghost Stories (Everyman's Library)

MORE BOSSINEY BOOKS ...

GHOSTS OF DORSET
by Peter Underwood
The President of the Ghost Club explored a whole range of Dorset hauntings. A ghostly white donkey, a world-famous screaming skull, phantom coach-and-horses story which Thomas Hardy used in *Tess of the D'Urbervilles* and a prehistoric 'Peeping Tom' are some of the subjects.
'*Ghost hunter Peter Underwood has been spook stalking in Dorset uncovering a host of eerie brushes with the supernatural.*'   Bournemouth Advertiser

STRANGE TALES OF THE SOUTH WEST
by Ronnie Hoyle
The South West is a natural breeding ground for strange tales. Well-known Westcountry journalist Ronnie Hoyle in his debut for Bossiney confirms this eerie fact.

KING ARTHUR IN THE WEST
by Felicity Young & Michael Williams
'*... brings together many of the strands in an exploration which takes them from Tintagel Castle and the Great Halls to Dunster and Dozmary, Glastonbury and so many other centres*'   The Western Morning News

SUPERSTITION AND FOLKLORE
by Michael Williams
A survey of Westcountry Superstitions: interviews on the subject and some Cornish and Devon folklore.
'*... the strictures that we all ignore at our peril. To help us to keep out of trouble, Mr Williams has prepared a comprehensive list.*'
Frank Kempe, North Devon Journal-Herald

GHOSTS OF DEVON
by Peter Underwood

GHOSTS OF CORNWALL
by Peter Underwood
'*A brilliant haunted double by the President of the Ghost Club Society, the man rated Britain's no.1 ghost hunter.*'

MYSTERIES OF THE SOUTH WEST
by Tamsin Thomas of BBC Radio Cornwall
A tour of ancient sites in Cornwall and on Dartmoor.
'*There is little doubt that Tamsin Thomas has become the 'Voice of Cornwall'.*'
North Cornwall Advertiser

PSYCHIC PHENOMENA OF THE WEST
by Michael Williams
'... *puts forward a cogent case for the supernatural. "Strange powers are at work in the west".'*
The Cornishman

LEGENDS OF DORSET
by Polly Lloyd
The author explores legendary Dorset, visiting places as diverse as the Sacred Circle at Knowlton and Chesil Beach. Dorset is a mine of myth and folklore.
'Weird happenings ... Polly Lloyd delves through tales ranging from moving rocks to murders.'
Ed Perkins, Southern Evening Echo

STRANGE STORIES FROM DEVON
by Rosemary Anne Lauder & Michael Williams. 45 photographs.
Strange shapes and places, strange characters, the man they couldn't hang, and a Salcombe mystery, the Lynmouth disaster and a mysterious house are some of the strange stories from Devon.
'... full of good stories, accompanied by many photographs of local happenings which have mystified.'
Mary Richards, Tavistock Times

ABOUT GLASTONBURY
by Polly Lloyd

PEOPLE & PLACES IN BRISTOL
introduced by E.V. Thompson

CURIOSITIES OF EXMOOR
by Felicity Young

SOMERSET MYSTERIES
by Polly Lloyd and Michael Williams

ABOUT EXMOOR
by Polly Lloyd

DARTMOOR REFLECTIONS
by David Mudd

We shall be pleased to send you our catalogue giving full details of our growing list of titles for Devon, Cornwall, Dorset, Somerset and Wiltshire and forthcoming publications. If you have difficulty in obtaining our titles, write direct to Bossiney, Books, Land's End, St Teath, Bodmin, Cornwall.